THE EURO-BANK

THE EURO-BANK
Its Origins, Management and Outlook

Steven I. Davis

Second Edition

To my mother and father for setting the example

First edition 1976
Second edition 1980

Published by
THE MACMILLAN PRESS LTD
London and Basingstoke
Companies and representatives
throughout the world

*Printed in Great Britain
by Redwood Burn Ltd
Trowbridge and Esher*

British Library Cataloguing in Publication Data

Davis, Steven I.
  The Euro-bank – 2nd ed.
  1. Banks and banking, International
  I. Title
  332.1'5   HG3881

ISBN 0–333–30003–3

Contents

Euro-ccy market   27-37→
outlook   136-8
                     143

v

Preface

Whereas I described my personal reactions on writing the first edition of this book four years ago as alternating between panic at stating the obvious and exhilaration at rediscovering the wheel, preparing the second edition provides another double-edged insight into both the performance of the Euro-banks and the validity of my own observations in mid-1975.

Whilst their market environment has shifted drastically from a relatively attractive risk/reward relationship for lending in the aftermath of the 1974 crisis of confidence to a highly competitive borrowers' market characterised by significant structural overcapacity, the Euro-banks as a market phenomenon have not only survived but also, in most cases, prospered to the extent that their profitability is generally competitive with that of their domestic parents. On the other hand, the intensity of competition and the increasing overlap of activities with parent organisations pose basic challenges which have resulted in the restructuring of a large number of Euro-banks.

In writing the second edition I have retained the basic structure of the first while updating all the statistical material and the interviews of senior Euro-bank executives, as well as taking advantage of new statistical series which have been made available since 1975. I have also made an effort to broaden the base of Euro-banks analysed from the exclusively London-based sample of four years ago by including a brief analysis of banks based in Hong Kong, Singapore and Luxembourg. A particular effort has been made throughout to analyse the changes which have taken place since 1975 and to present in the outlook section a more comprehensive and less tentative forecast than was possible in the first edition when the Euro-bank movement was largely in its adolescent stage of development.

I would like first to express once again my appreciation to T. M. Farmiloe of Macmillan Press and the banking colleagues, professors and friends who were instrumental in the conception and preparation of the first edition of this book. I am indebted to not only the senior executives of the 40 London-based banks but also the Asian bankers viii   *Preface*

whose comments in extensive confidential interviews provided the basis
for the bulk of Chapters 3, 4 and 5. Finally, a special word of thanks to
Sally Watts whose outstanding secretarial skills were complemented by
her research talent in updating the statistical tables.

London, October 1979   STEVEN I. DAVIS

Introduction and Overview

The purpose of this book, quite simply, is to analyse today's generation of Euro-banks from the perspective of management to determine how these banks are dealing with the critical issues they face at the end of the 1970s. The Euro-bond and Euro-currency markets centred in London have been the objects of extensive research and analysis by scholars, journalists and practitioners focusing on such sectors as economic theory and practice, market evolution and structure, and lending and investing practices. For an excellent coverage of these and other aspects of the Euro-markets, the reader is referred to volumes by Paul Einzig, Geoffrey Bell, Brian Scott Quinn and the Robert Morris Associates/Bankers' Association for Foreign Trade.[1]

Relatively little attention, however, has been devoted in the current literature to the separately capitalised, specialised banking institutions which have grown up with the market since the early 1960s. This book will attempt to describe some of the historical precedents for these institutions, the rationale for their establishment, their activities and objectives, and, in some detail, the conduct of asset and liability management as well as activities which do not relate directly to the balance sheet. There is nothing in this book that will significantly raise the learning curves of bankers active in the Euro-markets, but the consolidation in one volume of a body of management practices and the issues faced by Euro-bank management will hopefully have some value to those interested in management behaviour as well as the factors which will determine the future of these banks.

Euro-banks, rather than branches or other overseas operations of existing national banks, have been selected for analysis as their experience brings into focus more sharply many of today's issues in international banking because of the heavy concentration of their activity in the Euro-markets. While relatively unimportant in terms of market share, these banks in many respects are 'pure' international banks because of this Euro-market concentration. In addition, they are relatively free from the domestic influences which may dominate the behaviour of an overseas branch of an international bank. While this choice creates definitional problems which cannot be entirely resolved, the use of a sufficiently broad sample of Euro-banks should minimise these problems.

My focus throughout is on how management deals with the major issues confronting banks operating primarily in the Euro-currency market, and an attempt is made to define these issues. The book concludes with an effort to describe the factors which will influence Euro-banks in the future and to enumerate a few likely trends for Euro-banks individually as a market sector. As a by-product of the Euro-market boom of the 1960s and early 1970s, the Euro-bank in some cases was a fashionable, contemporary aspect of a national bank's overseas expansion programme; once established, however, most of these banks have developed a momentum and character of their own.

In addition to my own direct experience in the market since 1970, I have used as source material the bulk of the literature in English on the specific activities of international banks since the Middle Ages; recent books on Euro-market structure, theory and practice; and current statistical data published by international bodies such as the Bank for International Settlements and World Bank Group as well as such national authorities as the Federal Reserve Board and Bank of England. To supplement this data, I have also compiled statistics through 1978 on the financial performance of banks in London, Singapore, Hong Kong and Luxembourg to reflect actual management practice in terms of such key variables and measures of performance as gearing, asset composition, liquidity and return on assets and capital. Selecting both individual banks and financial centres inevitably involves making arbitrary distinctions. As defined later in this book, Euro-banks are separately capitalised international banks which were established or restructured since the mid-1960s largely to participate directly or indirectly in the Euro-markets based in London and other financial centres. In practice, they are generally owned by one or more financial institutions based in national banking markets. While conceptually the ideal Euro-bank carries on its own internationally-based business, in reality its ownership pattern and the use for regulatory and other factors of separately capitalised banks as proxies for branches of parent institutions means that the analyst must arbitrarily select for his Euro-bank sample institutions which have a *relative* identity separate from their parents as defined by their role in the interbank market, the presence of a separate loan portfolio, and so forth.

When the first edition of this book was written in 1975, I felt that the analytical portion could be centred only on Euro-banks whose major operational centre was London. London is not only the acknowledged international financial entrepôt in terms of size and depth, but also the operating base for a larger number of Euro-banks than any other market place. London-based banks tend to be older, larger and have a more meaningful statistical track record than those in newer centres such as Hong Kong, Singapore and Luxembourg. By 1979, however, a sufficiently large number of Euro-banks in each of these markets had evolved so that a London-based study could be supplemented by an analysis of patterns in these individual financial centres.

To the original statistical sample of forty London-based Euro-banks, therefore, I have added samples of eight banks each in these three markets. While such an extension of the analytical base inevitably dilutes somewhat the value of the analysis because of the specialist nature of several of these markets and the inclusion of even more institutions which are closer in nature to branches than self-standing Euro-banks, the global character of the Euro-markets ensures a certain comparability among what are still relatively pure international banking institutions.

Finally, to supplement my own personal management experience and views, in 1975 I conducted reasonably extensive interviews on management policies, issues and objectives with the senior management— generally the chief executive—of forty Euro-banks whose activities are conducted primarily in the London market. These were updated in mid-1979 discussions with the same individuals or their successors. With two exceptions, all the banks in the statistical sample are included in the interview sample. The results of these interviews must be qualified by the usual caveats applied to any 'on the record' comment dealing often with confidential information, but the assurance of anonymity to the interviewees and the emphasis on policy rather than confidential specifics discussed with a fellow banker hopefully produced some useful results.

More specifically, Chapter 1 provides a historical perspective for today's Euro-bank. While this is not an attempt to provide an authoritative, thorough history of international banking, an effort is made for three specific periods of international banking history to describe the structure, practice and objectives of new banks set up primarily to engage in international banking. A particular effort is made to focus on management practices of earlier institutions in terms of lending policies, types of borrowers, lending instruments, financial ratios, security obtained, loss experience, source of deposits and ultimate financial performance. Given the limited literature available on such micro-economic subjects, this analysis is necessarily spotty, but at a minimum the reader should be aware that today's generation of Euro-banks is not without historical precedents and that the experience of these antecedents may shed some light on the current operations and future of the Euro-banks.

Chapter 2 describes the development of the Euro-bank itself as an institution. Following a very brief summary of the evolution and structure of the Euro-currency markets, this chapter analyses the location, statistical importance, ownership, objectives, activities, and management background of the Euro-banking community.

The analysis of specific management policies is begun in Chapter 3, which centres on asset management. The principal asset components are described, and the relationship of the major categories of interbank loans and customer loans is analysed. Particular attention is paid to the management of the loan portfolio to maximise return and minimise losses. Such factors as risk diversification, credit standards, matur-ity controls, interest margin objectives, loan loss reserves, sources of business and decision making processes are analysed in some detail.

Chapter 4 focuses on liability, or money, management and capital adequacy. The importance and nature of deposits from other banks is studied in detail, and available data on the time mismatch between assets and liabilities are analysed. The decision-making process as it relates to the granting of interbank lines is discussed in the context of the vulnerability of a Euro-bank's deposits to loss of confidence in the market. The results of the 1974 crisis of confidence are studied in terms of parent support, differentiation of rates paid by banks, the different approaches taken to build a deposit base outside the interbank market, and the perceived need to participate in the market both as a lender and borrower of funds. The strategic role of a Euro-bank's dealing room is analysed along with the attitude toward dealing profitability and risk and the management controls placed on foreign exchange and deposit mismatch positions. Attitudes toward capital adequacy are discussed.

Non-deposit and lending operations are covered in Chapter 5, which discusses among others the investment or merchant banking activities Euro-banks have undertaken to improve their return on invested funds or carry out objectives established by parent banks. These include the management of syndicated loans, participation in the various aspects of the Euro-bond market or private placements of fixed interest obli-gations, corporate financial services, the taking of equity interests and other activities. Special attention is focused on the motivation of Euro-banks in deciding whether or not to undertake these non-commercial banking activities, the factors which appear to be vital for success, and the results obtained to date.

Chapter 6 examines the financial performance in recent years of samples of banks in the London, Singapore, Hong Kong and Luxembourg markets. On the basis of the published statements of these banks, the key ratios of gearing, liquidity, loans to deposits and capital funds and return on capital and assets are analysed. An attempt is made to relate performance to such factors as profitability goals stated by management in interviews and the profitability of non-Euro-banks.

The issues arising from Euro-bank experience to date are defined and discussed in Chapter 7. The boom period through mid-1974 is con-trasted with the sharp reversal of market conditions following the shocks to confidence experienced in the summer of 1974 with an emphasis on Euro-banks in particular. The increase in competition and deterioration of the lenders' risk/reward ratio in the period through 1979 are analysed. The problems of evaluation of international project and sovereign risk credits are reviewed together with the limited amount of information available with regard to actual loss experience to date. The issue of adequate funding is discussed in the context of the measures being taken to resolve the problem. The issue of providing an adequate return on invested funds is reviewed in the framework of the objectives of stockholders, and the contingent liability or responsibility on the part of the parent for the Euro-bank affiliate is discussed as a fourth issue. A final issue is the ability of Euro-banks to develop a significant investment banking or fee-based income.

The concluding chapter discusses the outlook for Euro-banks. A distinction is made between, on the one hand, the two exogenous factors of the development of the Euro-markets themselves and the status and priorities of individual parent institutions, and on the other, those factors which can be significantly influenced by management itself. Continued growth of the Euro-markets is projected although a slow-down in international trade and investment and periodic crises of confidence will influence Euro-bank development to a significant extent. The importance of management performance and profit record are emphasised. Stockholder attitudes in the context of actual performance and the ownership structure of the Euro-banks have and will continue to result in the restructuring of many Euro-banks, and the ability of stockholders to make a business contribution will be a major factor in determining future performance. Key factors by which management performance should be judged are discussed. Finally, a number of likely trends in range of services, profitability and physical location are reviewed.

1 Some Earlier Patterns in International Banking

The Euro-dollar market and the institutions it has spawned represent a unique phase of international banking development. There are, however, a number of periods since the Middle Ages when factors such as the growth of international trade and investment produced a variety of new banking institutions whose objectives, lending practices, market environment, sponsorship and structure were not at all dissimilar to the Euro-banks established in the 1960s and 1970s.

The behaviour of these institutions and their relative success in achieving objectives offer at a minimum a useful historical perspective with which to begin this book. The chapter which follows does not purport to be a throughgoing and fully researched history of international banking nor an intensive, systematic micro-analysis of banking behaviour through the ages. It does, however, summarise very roughly three periods of international banking history during which a novel combination of new banking institutions, financing techniques, or financial markets arose in response to a surge in cross-border lending and investment.

As available literature on the banking behaviour and policies which is our principal interest is quite limited, the following chapter has severe limitations from an analytical standpoint. It provides, however, a useful historical perspective for today's Euro-bank, particularly for the practitioner who is understandably fully involved in the challenges and opportunities of managing a Euro-bank in the early 1980s. For such a reader, no attempt has been made to draw parallels with contemporary experience, although Chapter 8 does relate some of the historical themes of international banking to today's problems. For the reader familiar with banking history and interested solely in current issues, however, an invitation is extended to commence one's reading with Chapter 2 of this book.

Renaissance Merchant Bankers: the Medici and Fugger

The fifteenth and sixteenth centuries in Europe witnessed the growth – and demise – of merchant banking dynasties who financed international trade, created foreign exchange markets, met the voracious financial needs of national rulers and the Papacy, and established new industrial and trade ventures. Starting from a slender capital base supplemented to a limited extent by deposits from the clergy and wealthy noblemen, these family-owned and managed banks grew through retained earnings to establish foreign subsidiaries and representative offices throughout Europe.

Given the proliferation of currencies – metal and paper, good and bad – and the religious prohibition against usury, the trade financing function in the fifteenth century almost inevitably involved a foreign exchange risk. Typically a Florentine bank lending to an Italian importing from England would buy from him for local currency a draft drawn in sterling on a London correspondent; the sterling proceeds would be used to purchase a bill on Florence to repay the lending bank. The selling rate of the initial bill would be fixed so that, at the then current exchange rate, the proceeds of the second bill would produce the desired interest return to the lender. If exchange rates changed in the three to four months needed to complete the transaction, either the banker or his borrower lost out. In addition to providing the necessary foreign exchange, such a transaction was not considered usury by the church as the lender was carrying a certain foreign exchange risk. In addition, the bank stood to lose money if the drawer of the initial bill would not pay, the correspondent bank failed to make the funds available, or if the remittance bill purchased was uncollectable.

The other traditional form of lending during this period was a short or medium-term direct extension of credit to an individual ruler, Pope, or member of the nobility or clergy. These were generally made on a fixed rate, fully secured basis with collateral consisting of jewels and other saleable personal assets, customs or tax receipts or the proceeds of sales of products such as copper or silver from royal or Papal monopolies.

In addition to their lending activities, the Renaissance merchant bankers sold goods on consignment and invested for their own account in the manufacture and shipment of commodities such as alum, wool, silk and spices. The Medici owned wool and silk factories which made a small contribution to overall profits, while about 20 per cent of the Fugger bank's assets in 1546 represented stock in trade of copper and cloth.[1] The Medici controlled partnerships which operated on a royalty basis the Papal alum mines at Tolfa and the iron mines on Elba, both of which represented regional monopolies.

Established in 1397 in Florence, the Medici Bank was the most important of its time, whereas Florence was the leading banking centre in the fourteenth and fifteenth centuries. Its larger predecessors in the fourteenth century – the Bardi and Peruzzi – had been liquidated following defaults on extensive loans to monarchs such as Edward III of England and Robert of Naples. Branches were established in the first half of the fifteenth century in Rome, Venice, Milan, Pisa, Avignon, Bruges, London and Geneva. Each branch was generally separately capitalised with funds provided by the local manager on a minority basis and the Medici family-controlled partnerships in Florence as majority stockholders. The local manager was compensated on a performance basis with a share of profits greater than his proportion of paid-in equity. This unique network functioned as an integrated unit by providing borrowing facilities to other branches, collecting remittances and drawing on other branches for trade financing requirements. Rome branch, which provided liquidity for the system by tapping Papal deposits, also provided over half the consolidated bank's profits during the early part of the fifteenth century.[2] Some deposits were also provided by wealthy individuals, who received interest on an 'as and when earned' basis to avoid charges of usury.

While no consolidated figures are available, it appears that non-stockholder deposits represented a multiple of up to ten times capital for individual branches. Fixed rate deposits could be acquired from money markets such as Antwerp on the basis of the Medici's prime name. Such deposits generally cost from 8–10 per cent per annum, while loans were made at rates of 12–14 per cent per annum. Overhead costs were minimal; in 1470 the entire network only employed fifty-seven individuals, or from four to ten per branch.[3] On the asset side of the ledger, cash rarely exceeded 10 per cent of total assets, with loans or claims on other Medici branches representing the bulk of the remainder.

Lending policy was established and generally enforced by guidelines laid down by the family and its general manager in Florence. Newly appointed branch managers signed contracts which, for example, required them to lend only to reputable merchants or manufacturers. Princes, noblemen and the clergy were generally considered bad risks except possibly on a cash collateralised basis. The new London manager in 1446 agreed not to accept bribes or lend to himself or his family, to give preference to other Medici branches in sending bills and goods on consignment and to insure goods sent by sea. Credit limits were established for other Italian banks and for individual members of the clergy from cardinal to the Pope, but no credit was to be extended to bankers in Genoa, Venice, Brittany or Gascony. At year end the manager would take the branch books to Florence for a thorough audit. All hiring was controlled by Florence to prevent collusion.

During the first half century of operation, under the management of Giovanni de Medici through Cosimo de Medici, earnings were quite satisfactory. The bank as a whole made 10 per cent on its capital in its first year of operations. A study of a series of typical exchange transactions shows that a median interest return of 14 per cent on foreign currency loans was achieved.[4] Some branches were remarkably successful; Venice's annual earnings for several years averaged 60 per cent of the branch capital, while those of Geneva exceeded 30 per cent of capital throughout the second quarter of the fifteenth century.

In 1464, however, the Bank entered into a serious state of decline due to a combination of external political and economic events, serious loan losses, stemming in large part from poor management in several branches, and increasingly ineffective control and direction from management in Florence. Wars or other political conflicts involving Florence had serious repercussions on the viability of individual branches; French kings on several occasions forced the Lyons branch to close down or modify its policies, while Venice and Naples suffered from regional warfare. An imbalance of trade between Northern and Southern Europe severely restrained the financing of trade; exports from the north were dependent upon English wool, which was in short supply for economic reasons as well as English efforts to restrict the export of raw wool.

Loans to monarchs, often against the express policy of home office, produced massive losses, although in many branches the local ruler represented the only reasonably creditworthy borrower. The Milan branch was established as a gesture of support to the Duke of Milan, the Medici's political ally. Within eight years of its establishment, loans to the Duke and Duchess represented 37 per cent of total assets and 168 per cent of the branch's capital.[5] In London, loans to Edward IV represented the principal means of obtaining permission to export wool so as to provide remittances to cover English imports. Eventually over four times the branch's capital was lent to Edward, and the cost of borrowed funds to carry these non-accruing loans coupled with the periodic defaults stemming from the War of the Roses ate up the branch's profits. The Bruges manager far exceeded his established limit to Charles the Bold of Burgundy; over four times the branch's capital was outstanding to the Duke at the time of his death. Invariably these branch managers found themselves lending new funds to heads of state to recoup existing loans.

During the final years of the Medici Bank culminating in the expulsion of the Medici from Florence in 1494, the head office management under Lorenzo de Medici and his general manager, Sassetti, actively closed down unprofitable branches, mobilised cash resources and tried with limited success to control their branch managers. Loan losses of a multiple of capital in several branches, coupled with low cash reserves and the external political and economic factors mentioned above led, however, to the gradual liquidation of individual branches and the bank's ultimate demise. Even the once profitable Rome branch was liquidated after the Pope for political reasons repudiated his debts to the Medici and cancelled the alum contract. A recalcitrant manager in Lyons finally had to be jailed after losing a multiple of the branch's capital because of bad loans and stale merchandise stocks. Professor de Roover concludes that 'Techniques have changed, but human problems have remained the same. How to pick out the right person and put him in the right place was as much a problem for the Medici as it is in business today.'[6] With regard to lending policy, he notes that the 'congenital defect of . . . the financial type of sedentary merchant to drift from private banking into government finance'[7] made a major contribution to the Medici collapse.

The decline and fall of the Florentine merchant bankers was followed in the sixteenth century by a similar era of dominance by South German bankers led by the Fugger family as well as the development of sophisticated international money markets in centres such as Antwerp and Lyons.

Antwerp and other money centres were unregulated markets where private bankers traded commodities, engaged in money trading in the form of the purchase and sale of bills of exchange, and made short term direct loans to banks and governments. On the Antwerp Bourse loans of three to six months at interest rates of 8–12 per cent (depending on the credit) were made to banks like Fugger by other banks and wealthy individuals. Loans to governments, with or without guarantees by banks or well regarded subjects such as the City of Antwerp, were traded in the form of certificates at rates reflecting the borrower's credit record. In the 1540s and 1550s, the English government generally paid approximately 12 per cent per annum for its funds, while Spain would often pay a 16 per cent interest rate.[8] Rates paid would vary not only on the basis of the name of the royal borrower but also the quality of security or outside guarantee. Government loans syndicated among a number of Antwerp and Lyons banks of which one, the agent, held the collateral, were prevalent. In 1555, the French government issued the 'Grand Parti', a ten-year loan consolidating outstanding loans plus a certain amount of new money at a relatively high 16 per cent; the large number of individuals who rushed to participate in the loan were disappointed when the loan defaulted two years later.

The Fugger bank owes its ascent and collapse to the Habsburg family which it financed during the sixteenth and early seventeenth centuries. Direct loans to monarchs such as Maximilian and Charles V were initially made on a secured basis for a one-year maturity at a rate of 12–14 per cent per annum; these loans were financed by matching money market deposits on which interest at 8–10 per cent per annum was charged to Fugger as a prime borrowing name. Loans for purely political purposes were common; in 1530, to elect Charles V's brother as King of Rome, the Fugger made a 275,000 florin eight-year loan at 10 per cent interest secured by various official revenues with a front end fee of 40,000 florins, or 15 per cent of the principal amount, as a 'special refreshment and token of honor'.[9] Capital funds and deposits by the Fugger family usually represented the bulk of the balance sheet, with borrowings in the Antwerp Bourse representing the largest portion of external liabilities. In addition to loans, assets were made up of holdings of land, mines and commodities held for their own account.

Being imperial banker to an empire struggling to conquer the Low Countries and financed ultimately through precious metals from the New World was profitable but involved an increasing concentration of risk. In the seven years to 1546, for example, the Fugger bank earned an annual average of 19 per cent per annum on invested capital. On the other hand, direct and indirect loans to the Habsburg Emperor represented not only an increasing proportion of total assets but also a substantial source of loan write-offs. In 1546, loans to the Emperor represented 2 million florins, or 28 per cent of total assets of 7.1 million florins and over half the entire loan portfolio; on the liability side, net worth represented 5.1 million florins and liabilities, mostly bills borrowed on the Antwerp market, 2 million florins.[10]

The bank increasingly found itself lending new funds to protect existing loans to the Habsburgs; collateral consisted of pledged tax receipts in the Netherlands or Spain which often were not forthcoming. Against a capital (reduced by loan losses) of 2 million florins, loans to the Habsburgs rose to 4.5 million florins in 1563. After a series of agreed moratoria and official Spanish bankruptcies during which interest rates were reduced and maturities extended, about 8 million Rhenish gulders of Habsburg loans were finally written off in 1650, thereby wiping out most of the bank's earnings over the previous century.[11]

Merchant and Investment Banks During the Nineteenth Century

Between the Napoleonic wars and the late nineteenth century, international trade and investment flourished under the stimulus of capital exports and trade finance supplied by the London and Paris financial markets. Despite periodic economic crises during the period stemming from occasional commodity price collapses, over-extension of credit and financial panics, an apparently irresistible urge to invest European capital abroad brought forth waves of new financial institutions. Most of these new banks collapsed in the wake of the century's recurrent slumps and panics, but a number survived to become some of today's leading financial institutions. In the analysis which follows, particular attention will be placed on the qualities which appear to differentiate the new international banks which survived from those which disappeared.

The new international banks in the nineteenth century were engaged in two fundamentally different activities: investment banking, or the arrangement on an agency or underwriting basis of long-term funds for infrastructural and industrial development, and trade financing on the traditional basis of the bill drawn, usually on London, to finance commodity exports and imports. Both sectors had their share of casualties.

Typical of the trade financing, or commercial lending, enterprises was that of Baring Brothers' activities in financing US trade with England.[12] On the strength of its close correspondent ties in America and the relative cheapness of the London money market, Barings offered lines of credit to American commodity exporters and commercial houses interested in drawing sterling bills on London to finance trade or to deal in foreign exchange. As London correspondent of the Bank of the United States, it functioned for a certain period as the semi-official London banker to the US government. With interest rates in the early 1830s of $5\frac{1}{2}$–7 per cent per annum in the US and $2\frac{3}{4}$–$3\frac{3}{4}$ per cent in London, the latter naturally was an attractive financing market, and the United States soon became the most highly regarded credit risk outside England in the 1830s.

From a limited capital base of £492,000 in 1830, Barings operated profitably throughout the century with a minimal loss record despite the series of public and private defaults, bank failures and commodity price collapses which marked the period. Supported by good economic intelligence and credit files contained in its 'Private Remarks Book', Barings was able to contract its outstanding short-term bill obligations or insist on additional security when it sensed an approaching crisis. Clean advances were made against the shipment of commodities with an appropriate margin; only second-line credits, which were in the minority, required additional security in the form of documents. Consignment business was emphasised; Barings charged 2½ per cent to sell consigned merchandise and 1 per cent as agent to market US securities. No loans in excess of the borrower's capital were permitted, and the bank generally required that all of a customer's financing be done through Barings. Interest on outstandings was usually debited at a rate of 5 per cent, while credit balances with Barings generally earned 4 per cent interest.[13] Of all the major Anglo-American financing houses, only Barings survived the 1837 crisis and commodity price collapse without assistance from the Bank of England.

Whereas Barings operated only through a representative in the United States, a number of British-owned banks were established with a network of foreign branches to exploit trade with particular commodity-rich areas such as Latin America and South Africa. Control of these banks was exerted through a board of senior management in London, where the money market was used as a source of short-term finance to cover the debit balances of the overseas branches.

In Latin America, the predecessors of the Bank of London and South America survived the sharp commodity price fluctuations, public and private defaults and civil strife of the mid-nineteenth century.[14] Managers of BOLSA branches were instructed to finance only short-term trade movements which were self-liquidating in nature, not crops in the ground. Loans to governments or against mortgages or other securities were generally prohibited. Loans and deposits were matched on a currency basis despite the temptation to convert sterling deposits and lend the higher yielding local currencies, and liquidity in the form of cash normally represented one-third of the branches' deposits. In South Africa, the Standard Bank from its establishment in 1863 also concentrated on commodity financing despite the attractions of other forms of lending.[15] Wool, gold and diamond exports were financed, despite some losses due to the collapse of prices in the 1860s and 1880s. While some losses were suffered on loans against mining shares and claims, the general policy of lending against the commodities themselves was a major factor in the survival of the bank.

A unique phenomenon of the nineteenth century was the development of investment banking institutions such as the Rothschild bank, the Crédit Mobilier and geographically specialised banks whose principal activity was the intermediation of long-term capital exports from England and France. Undeterred by depressingly regular defaults by private and public overseas borrowers, the British and French public through their bankers financed a world-wide programme of infrastructure and industry – railroads, canals, public utilities, mines and factories – through term debt and equity issues floated in London and Paris. The banks placed the funds either as agent or on an underwriting basis. Issues were priced at a discount from par with the underwriter seeking to obtain the major portion of his compensation from an increase over the offering price. In many cases, banks promoted new overseas ventures, retained an equity stake and maintained a market in the venture's publicly-held securities.

Among the more successful investment banks of the period, the Rothschilds operated throughout most of the nineteenth century as a single firm with branches in Paris, London, Vienna and Frankfurt, each managed by a member of the family. Close political connections with the rulers of the time were utilised to prevent wars which could jeopardise their various interests; Prince Metternich's right-hand man in the early part of the century, Frederick von Gentz, was actually a salaried employee of the Rothschilds.[16] The bank initiated the Continental railroad building boom in 1835 by obtaining the Nordbahn concession from the Austrian government. In Spain, to obtain the European quicksilver monopoly, they bid in 1835 for the same concession owned in the sixteenth century by the Fugger; the bid succeeded at least in part because of a simultaneous loan and gifts to the financially hard-pressed Spanish government.[17] Political as well as economic conditions were attached to the loans which were granted to virtually all major European countries; a railroad credit to King Leopold of Belgium in 1837 was granted on the condition, among others, that he suppress a potential revolutionary movement in Luxembourg, and that no further disbursements should take place if war were to break out.[18] Rivalry with the Crédit Mobilier for control of a European railroad network led to an aggressive campaign of bids and takeovers which terminated in the Rothschilds' obtaining control of the northern Italian railway system just before the Italian war of independence against Austria. Profits appear to have been generated by gains on the sale of stock of the ventures it promoted as well as fees earned through the flotation of government loans, although losses suffered on securities held during the

European wars of the 1860–71 period must have been substantial.

Established in Paris in 1852 by the Pereire brothers and the Fould bank, the Crédit Mobilier represented the first institutional attempt to tap private savings on a major scale through a joint-stock company for capital investment outside France.[19] A network of affiliated investment banks was set up in England (International Financial Society Limited), Spain (Credito Mobiliario Espanol), Germany (Darmstadter Bank), Italy (Credito Mobiliare Italiano), and Holland (Crédit Neerlandais). Activity was directed initially toward the promotion, construction and acquisition of railroads financed by Crédit Mobilier bond issues, usually in competition with the Rothschild bank. Imitators of the Crédit Mobilier sprang up throughout Europe; four were established in Spain alone in the 1850s, with the result that 80 per cent of railway trackage in Spain in 1861 belonged to French-controlled companies.[20] In practice, the Crédit Mobilier was prepared to lend for a longer period against riskier securities than would be accepted by a commercial bank.

Earnings were derived primarily from the promotion of new ventures, generally through the sale of shares sold at a premium after the initial offering. While it contributed 40 per cent of the 650 million francs total capital of the foreign banks it helped found, its own capital for most of the fifteen years of its life did not exceed a fairly modest sixty million francs.[21] While its flexibility and aggressiveness created a number of highly successful financial institutions and projects, it suffered heavy losses as the result of the collapse of its Dutch bank and its railroads in Russia and Switzerland. A loan to finance Maximilian's expedition to Mexico may also have contributed to the Crédit Mobilier's demise in 1867, when the Pereire brothers left the bank and its various emanations were liquidated or acquired by outside interests. In retrospect, inadequate project analysis, which led to substantial cost overruns and inadequate revenues for the projects financed by the Crédit Mobilier, also was a factor in its disappearance.

Such was the unprecedented enthusiasm on the part of British and French individual investors for the higher yields and glamour of foreign securities that 'Any government which claimed sovereignty over a bit of the earth's surface and a fraction of its inhabitants could find a financial agent in London and purchasers for her bonds.'[22]

With foreign government and infrastructure or railway bonds effectively yielding $5\frac{1}{2}$–8 per cent per annum compared to British Consols at 3–4 per cent, the supply of funds was vast and the borrowers responded enthusiastically. Investment banks in London and Paris and the newly-formed overseas banks would compete vigorously for an exclusive mandate to raise funds for a given government or to establish a railway or mineral concession. With such a mandate usually came the profitable remittance, cash management and agency business for that borrower. On either a best efforts or underwritten basis, the issue would be placed with individual investors in Europe through the major clearing and deposit banks in England, France and Germany. In the 1820s, management or underwriting fees amounted to 2–5 per cent of the nominal amount of the loan (usually far in excess of the issue price) and additional profits were earned by agency fees, the use of free balances and the manipulation of the market price by placing forward purchase orders to insure an opening premium over the offering price.[23] For the latter purpose, the proceeds of the loan itself were often used to create a premium which would attract additional buyers. Bonds were often allocated to banks at a price below the price to the public as a form of compensation.

The peak of the foreign-bond mania and the banking expansion which accompanied it was reached in the late 1870s. 'No country was so willing as England to expand credit beyond the limits of commercial prudence.'[24] Not only were less developed countries (Russia, Turkey, Spain, Egypt, a host of Latin American countries) and high risk start-up projects (a variety of US, Latin American and European railways) financed, but lack of due diligence brought to the market a number of fraudulent or imaginary offerings. Gregor MacGregor, a Scottish adventurer, persuaded a London house whose principal was a former Lord Mayor of London to bring to market a £200,000 loan to the State of Poyais, an imaginary state on the Mosquito Coast of Nicaragua, which was convertible into freehold land in 'Poyais'.[25] Notwithstanding the death of colonists who unwittingly set out for Poyais, MacGregor was able two years later to perform the same feat with another London house for another imaginary kingdom. The railway boom was such that a promotion in the US by the name of the Atlantic and Great Western Railroad, which was to run between the metropoli of Salamanca, New York and Dayton, Ohio, was able in 1865 to borrow its entire capitalisation, including rolled up interest, in the London market without a penny of equity invested.[26]

The default record on these borrowings, while painful, did not deter individual European investors for long. In 1841–2 nine US states suspended interest payments, and in subsequent years approximately one-half of the US railroads went into receivership. In 1873–4 alone, the governments of Honduras, Costa Rica, Santo Domingo, Paraguay, Spain, Egypt, Turkey, Peru, Uruguay, Liberia, Guatemala and Bolivia defaulted, often because the fear generated by the contemporary wave of defaults prevented otherwise creditworthy countries from refinancing existing obligations.[27]

The premium yield on overseas securities and the enthusiasm for commodity wealth abroad led to the establishment at mid-century of dozens of banks specialising in exporting British and French funds to specific less developed regions with apparent economic potential. Apart from the banks discussed above, the Near and Far East as well as Europe and North and South America attracted banks promoted and often controlled by London and Parisian financial groups. Most of these promotions either never opened their doors or closed within a few years due to massive loan losses.

The end of the Crimean War and the obvious capital requirements of the Turkish Empire led to the establishment of promotions such as the Bank of Egypt in 1855, which was sponsored by some leading London bankers and was the first British joint stock bank to commence business abroad.[28] Operating with branches in Egypt and a head office in London, its management guidelines forbade land speculation, placed a ceiling on loans to directors of one-third of the total and limited the issue of its notes to three times capital plus the bullion reserve. As in the case of most banks of its kind, however, its loan portfolio was tied to the fortunes of the Egyptian economy – primarily cotton – and the credit-worthiness of the local ruler. Following some early losses and the ejection of the individual who had promoted and managed the bank, it paid a dividend of 10–20 per cent on its capital through the 1860s and 1870s but finally collapsed following the 1907 crisis when half of its acceptance liabilities proved uncollectable.

The Anglo-Egyptian Bank, a competitor established in 1864 by two major British banks, was rescued by the Egyptian Viceroy himself, who voluntarily took up half of the bank's share of a sticky government loan underwritten by Anglo-Egyptian and made an *ex gratia* payment to compensate the bank for its loss on the remainder.[29]

The capital requirements of Turkey itself attracted a variety of new institutions promoted by British and French banks, of which the Imperial Ottoman Bank was the principal survivor. With British investors owning over half the issued capital, the bank assumed quasi-central banking status through the issue of notes and collection of tax revenues. Substantial earnings were realised on foreign exchange dealings, and the bank not only survived the Turkish government's defaults in the 1870s but was usually able to pay a 12 per cent dividend on capital funds.

In North America, a total of five British-owned banks were operating in California alone in the 1860s; activities included dealing in bullion, advances on merchandise and securities and the sale of sterling bills. One of these banks, the London and San Francisco Bank, was owned by ten British and ten German banks and was finally acquired in 1905 by the Bank of California.

In the Far East, the scene of an active three-cornered trade among China, India and England, a grand total of twenty-two newly established Anglo-Eastern banks on the brink of liquidation were dealt a final blow as the result of the 1866 financial crisis associated with the crash of Overend Gurney.[30] The first British-owned bank in the Far East, the Oriental Banking Corporation, survived the 1866 crisis but was liquidated towards the end of the century following the collapse of silver prices on which the Far Eastern economy was based. The principal survivor of these banks was the Hong Kong and Shanghai Banking Corporation, which survived not only the 1866 crash, civil strife in China, bad debts in Hong Kong but also losses in the London office through the unauthorised purchase of US bonds. Loans were generally made in silver and tied to foreign trade, and substantial foreign exchange profits were realised.

Towards the end of the century the British and French overseas banks were joined by offshore subsidiaries established by the major German mixed banks. The 1870s saw the establishment in London of banks such as the London and Hanseatic Bank (Commerzbank) and German Bank of London (Deutsche Bank).

In Europe itself, a host of consortium institutions had a brief but eventful life in the 1860s. The Anglo-Italian Bank was set up by such leading English bankers as George Peabody & Co. in 1864 to introduce English banking techniques to Italy. While the directors believed that 'by lending money to public establishments for a longer period than was usual in [England] and making advances to municipalities on the security of the rates, [the Directors] had reason to believe a safe and profitable business might be secured.'[31] Within a few years, exchange losses resulted in the write-off of over half the bank's capital. The English and Swedish Bank, run by English bankers, survived three years; the Madrid Bank in Spain lasted two years before being wound up. At least three British-owned banks set up in Russia had disappeared by 1871.

To the normal risks of war and political conflict, violent fluctuations of commodity prices and mal-administration of less developed economies and political systems was thus added in the nineteenth century an overwhelming and relentless appetite for foreign securities which was sustained, if not whetted, by the activities of individual promoters and newly established specialist international banks. While it is difficult to generalise on the basis of available information, it would appear that the demise of so many new institutions is attributable as much to poor and inexperienced management in the form of over-concentration of credit, mismatching of lending and borrowing currencies, lack of analysis and overenthusiasm in a complex environment as to the external factors mentioned. There would also appear to have been a greater mortality rate among overseas subsidiary banks which were less tightly controlled from home office than branches. In any case, over half the new international banks promoted between 1856 and 1865 aborted, and over a quarter of the promotions which were actually set up were insolvent within five years.[32]

Despite these disappointments, about £3.8 billion in foreign long term publicly issued capital was held by British investors in 1913; this represented about 25 per cent of Britain's Gross National Product and roughly 10 per cent of the country's net income.[33] While the proportion of French GNP invested abroad was somewhat less, a total of 109 foreign securities were quoted in 1869 on the Paris Bourse. Thanks in large part to the efforts of the international investment banks, Latin America owed foreign investors about $6,000 million by 1913, and Russia had become the largest European borrower on the eve of the Revolution.[34]

US Commercial Bank Expansion in the Early Twentieth Century

One of the most interesting episodes of the development of international banking is the burst of expansion abroad by American commercial banks during the period beginning with World War I and continuing during the 1920s. As in the case of so many other banks before them who moved quickly into new markets with significant political and economical risks, mistakes were made and substantial write-offs of loans and equity investments affected American bank profit and loss statements in the 1920s and 1930s.

Until 1913 international banking had been dominated by the European-controlled overseas or colonial banks as a consequence of the export of European capital in the nineteenth century. In 1910, for example, there were thirty-two British colonial banks headquartered in London with 2104 branches in the colonies in addition to eighteen other

British-owned foreign banks with 175 branches.[35] Eighteen French colonial banks had 104 offices, and German and Dutch banks operated somewhat smaller networks.

The passage of the Federal Reserve Act in 1913, coupled with the outbreak of World War I which was to turn the United States from the world's largest debtor nation into a major creditor, precipitated a rapid expansion of foreign branches and subsidiaries of American banks. While a few consortium-owned subsidiary banks had been established under state laws in earlier years, the Federal Reserve Act permitted national banks to branch abroad and to accept drafts for the first time. The dollar acceptance thus came to play a major role at the expense of the sterling draft drawn on a country which had been hard hit by the war and whose post war balance of payments vulnerability was to severely restrict its former role as the world's banker.

US banks moved abroad initially through branches or subsidiaries which themselves branched abroad. Six consortium subsidiaries were incorporated under state law and included:

(1) American Foreign Banking Corporation, which was incorporated in 1917 by over thirty banks in America and Canada, established seventeen foreign branches in Latin America and Europe. The Chase Bank, which was one of the stockholders, acquired its three remaining branches in 1925.

(2) Asia Banking Corporation, incorporated in 1918 and owned by the Guaranty Trust Company, Continental Bank of Chicago and other US banks, opened eleven foreign branches in the Far East and San Francisco. Following a voluntary liquidation in 1924, its remaining assets were bought up by a subsidiary of the National City Bank.

(3) Mercantile Bank of the Americas, which was established in 1915 with a capital of $11 million by Brown Brothers, Guaranty Trust and other US interests; it rapidly opened branches in Europe and established controlled subsidiaries in Peru, Venezuela, Columbia, Brazil, Cuba, Costa Rica, Nicaragua and Honduras. At its zenith the bank had forty-five overseas offices. The collapse of commodity prices in 1920 forced a reorganisation of the bank in 1922 as the Bank of Central and South America; the bank's Havana office alone lent $25 million against sugar which dropped in price from $.21 to $.02 per pound. Despite the stockholder support of the banks such as J. P. Morgan, Guaranty Trust, Seligman, Corn Exchange and W. R. Grace, the new bank, which operated twenty-two foreign offices, was sold three years later to the Royal Bank of Canada.

(4) Park-Union Foreign Banking Corporation was set up in 1919 by the
     National Park Bank of New York and the Union Bank of Canada to
     finance trade with the Far East through branches in Japan, China
     and Paris. It went into voluntary liquidation in 1922.

At their zenith, the foreign banking subsidiaries operated eighty-one
overseas branches.[36] By 1927, however, all the remaining consortium-
owned foreign banking subsidiaries had been absorbed by US banks.
Companies established under the new Edge Act, passed in 1919, fared no
better. All three formed in the early 1920s, including one consortium
with 1000 banking stockholders, disappeared by 1933. Of the eighteen
banking corporations – Edge Act and Agreement – which initially came
under the Federal Reserve's jurisdiction, only three survived beyond the
early 1930s.

The failure of these new ventures sponsored by major US banking
institutions has been attributed to a combination of inexperienced
management, over-rapid expansion, the 1920 foreign trade crisis,
excessive eagerness and competition for business, conflicts among the
banking stockholders and the usual problems of doing business in
countries with a significant degree of political instability and vulnerability to commodity price fluctuation. In several cases parent banks
began to perform the same functions as their subsidiaries. While the
consortium approach clearly limited the exposure of individual banks,
'it soon appeared that the bank stockholders in such institutions were
inclined to suspect one another or to fear that through some lack of
loyalty one or the other of them would be disadvantaged'.[37] The lack of
experience of American bankers was blamed:

> the expansion was unduly rapid and unwarranted; trained men for the
> management of foreign banks were lacking . . . It is by this long
> drawn out method that British and Canadian banks have built up the
> personnel of their foreign branches, and there seems to be no shorter
> road to real success in overseas banking.[38]

The ultimate fate of the early consortium banks was liquidation,
absorption of assets by one or more of the stockholders, or sale of assets
to another bank.

Branch banking by organisations such as National City Bank, Chase,
Morgan, and First of Boston produced more positive results in Latin
America, Asia and Europe. From a total of twenty-six foreign offices in
1916, the total (including branches of subsidiaries) rose to 181 in 1920,

although it fell back in 1926 to 107 primarily as a result of the liquidation of subsidiary banks. The National City Bank alone in 1926 had a world-wide network of fifty-one direct branches in addition to the twenty-two branches of its wholly-owned subsidiary.

US corporate investment and commodity imports encouraged the establishment of a number of US branches throughout Latin America, although the periodic collapse of commodity prices caused many sleepless nights for bankers. With an estimated $1200 million lent to Latin American borrowers by 1929, the price collapse of 1930 and subsequent widespread defaults had a significant impact on American banks. The drop in sugar prices in 1921 from 22 cents to 3.5 cents per pound resulted in US banks taking over and running Cuban plantations and mills as well as writing off substantial loans. When commodity prices dropped again in 1930, the banks were better prepared and had begun to insist on such safeguards as earlier repayment and prior sale of sugar to an ultimate buyer or on the futures market. Throughout the inter-war period, support to South American countries in payments difficulties was provided by guarantees from the US Export-Import Bank. American bankers in Latin America were accused of lack of sound banking judgement, overexpansion, cutting lending rates and lack of understanding of the nature of one or two crop economies.

Other branches were located in London and Paris to perform securities arbitrage, handle foreign exchange transactions and service US corporations in Europe. In Asia, the branches of US banks with their more conservative policies succeeded where the consortium banks had failed; profits were made on immigrant remittances, loans against gold and silver, and trade financing.

Somewhat chastened by their mixed experience in Latin America, US banks turned to European borrowers which traditionally had enjoyed the best credit ratings. The ravages of the war and subsequent inflation had, however, somewhat damaged these ratings. The onslaught of foreign banks continued during the 1920s:

Not only American and English but also Dutch, Swiss, Swedish and French banks and issuing houses approached foreign states, cities, railroads, public utilities and industrial corporations, offering them loans and credits without serious concern as to their ability to repay in the lender's currency.[39]

The lack of any international co-ordination in lending to Central

European countries, the collapse of the New York Stock Exchange and the consequent check to the outflow of loan funds and the tariff barriers placed on European exports finally culminated in 1931 in the collapse of key Central European banks and the standstill agreement on German short term debt to foreign creditors. Germany had enjoyed a top credit rating before the war, and the US bankers were attracted by the higher rates paid by German banks and corporations on short-term, presumably self-liquidating, acceptance financing. As a partner in Kuhn Loeb put it during a 1931 Senate investigation,

> England . . . had an age-old prestige for judgement and wisdom in the matter of international financial borrowings. We were perfectly justified in following . . . the example of a wise old nation like England, being right there, and a wise old nation like Holland . . . who, in proportion to their resources, gave larger short term credits to Germany than America did . . . It may be locked up for a while, yes, but that is the ordinary risk of business.[40]

In total, Germany owed its foreign bank creditors an estimated $1000 million of which US banks held about $600 million in short term credits. One US bank was reported to have had $130 million outstanding to Germany in 1931. When US banks began in March 1931 to pull back their short term credits to foreigners, roughly 40 per cent of US short term claims were on German borrowers. According to Thomas Lamont's testimony before the Senate, about ninety US banks were lending to Germany; as of November 1932, about $500 million in short term credit was held by thirty New York banks and twenty-eight interior banks.[41] Standstill agreements under which US banks agreed to maintain outstanding credit were extended on an annual basis until World War II; from time to time portions of the dollar debt were converted into marks which could be sold at a discount, used to acquire German assets or held in blocked accounts. The steady depreciation of the mark, however, ultimately resulted in substantial write-offs on the books of American banks. Similar standstill agreements for smaller amounts of bank loans were agreed with Austria and Hungary.

By the end of 1933, when hundreds of banks around the world had closed their doors permanently, 67 per cent of the Latin American and 46 per cent of the European-issued dollar bonds were in default as to interest. A US government report summed up the overseas lending activities in the 1920s as follows:

Under the high pressure salesmanship methods by which foreign issues were solicited and sold, our loans proved to be their undoing. The flotation of one loan frequently came to be regarded as adequate justification for further issues to the same borrower or the same country without regard to the growing burden of indebtedness.[42]

2 The Evolution and Description of the Euro-Bank

As has happened so often in the history of international banking, a massive and sustained growth in overseas trade and investment has brought forth a new generation of international financial institutions during the past fifteen years. The period since the end of World War II has witnessed an unprecedented internationalisation of the world's economies in the context of an equally remarkable rate of overall economic growth. What has particularly marked this post-war period of international banking growth has been the evolution of a network of sophisticated markets in foreign currency loans and deposits with an ease of access that has permitted the emergence of new banking institutions which otherwise might not have seen the light of day.

It is this new generation of banks which is the subject of this book. The significance of the Euro-bank lies less in its physical importance than in the fact that it approximates a 'pure' international bank in microcosm without the domestic base which characterises other institutions whose international activity may be much larger in absolute terms. Recognising that any definition in such a large and varied banking community as the Euro-currency market must necessarily be imprecise, I have defined a Euro-bank to be an international banking institution with its own capital base, a certain degree of management autonomy, executive offices in London or another international finance centre, and whose principal activity is related directly or indirectly to the taking of deposits in Euro-currencies (currencies held outside their national market) and on-lending them to customers or other banks. A large number of Euro-banks also participate actively in various aspects of the Euro-bond market. While a number of common characteristics exist between Euro-banks and overseas branches of American and other national banks, the former usually develop a special identity because of factors such as their separate management structure, own capitalisation and need to attract funds under their own name.

In most cases, these banks have been established by other financial institutions since the mid-1960s specifically to operate in the Euro-currency and Euro-bond markets. Ownership structures range from the wholly-owned subsidiary to consortium banks with a dozen or more stockholders. While their objectives, sponsorship, structures and size may vary significantly, they generally derive most of their earnings from interest income and fund themselves primarily in the interbank market. Their principal centre of operations tends to be in one of the international money market centres such as London, Luxembourg or Singapore, although for tax or administrative reasons they may be incorporated elsewhere. The analytical focus in this book is on London-based Euro-banks in view of their relative importance in size and number, the availability of published information and the dominance of London as the principal international financial market. On the other hand, the management issues discussed should be equally relevant to Euro-banks in centres such as Singapore, Luxembourg and Hong Kong.

The history, structure, theory and practice of the Euro-markets have been described in some detail in a number of excellent volumes and articles, and the purpose of this book is not to duplicate what has already been written on these subjects. A few brief paragraphs on the nature and structure of the Euro-currency market, however, may provide a useful introduction to a discussion of the Euro-banks themselves.

The market for Euro-currencies (defined as dollars and other leading currencies deposited in banks other than those of the country where these currencies are issued) grew up in the late 1950s and 1960s primarily in response to the rapid and sustained expansion of international trade and investment, the large US balance of payments deficits which financed a good portion of this expansion, and various national – principally American – exchange, interest rate and reserve requirement regulations which encouraged the development of an unregulated international money market where funds could flow freely in response to supply and demand. As measured by the Bank for International Settlements (BIS), which includes the outstanding amount of foreign currency credits channelled through the nine European countries covered by its statistics but excludes interbank lending within a given country and lending to local institutions, the Euro-currency market grew at an amazing compound annual rate of 26.7 per cent between 1970 and 1978 to reach a gross level at December 1978 of $502,000 million in assets.[1]

Approximately 25 per cent of these funds were on-lent to non-bank customers. At end-1978 the dollar component of these assets was 68 per cent of the total, as against 73 per cent at the end of 1974, reflecting the growth in importance of the Deutsche Mark and other currencies. If one were to include non-European markets such as the Bahamas, Panama, Tokyo, Canada and Singapore, the size of the world Euro-currency market at end-1978 (including domestic interbank and other lending of foreign currencies) has been estimated by Morgan Guaranty Trust Company to be approximately $890,000 million.[2]

Table A shows an estimated breakdown of the gross market by David Ashby published in the *Investors' Chronicle* in September 1979. While no direct comparison with national markets is possible, it is interesting to note that in mid-1979, *The Economist* estimated that the net size of the market at about $500 billion represented one-fifth of the combined money stocks of the seven major industrial countries (the US, Canada, Japan, France, West Germany, Italy and Britain).[3]

In achieving this impressive year-to-year growth, which was only interrupted briefly in mid-1974, the market has consistently confounded observers who predicted its demise because of such concerns as lack of confidence, the imposition of controls, the opening up of the US market in 1974 when exchange controls were lifted, the by-passing of the market by OPEC funds, and a domino-like collapse stemming from borrower defaults. Innovation and flexibility have characterised the Euro-currency market, which has developed new loan pricing techniques, tapped new sources of funds, located new borrowers and developed loan syndication techniques which did not exist fifteen years ago.

While the market originated and is still centred in London, satellite markets throughout the world have grown up where foreign currency deposits are traded among banks. According to Ashby's data, the London market comprises somewhat under one-third of the world-wide total. American banks, which represent the single largest factor in the Euro-currency market, hold about one-third of their foreign branch deposits in London[4], while the United Kingdom represents somewhat less than one half of the foreign currency assets in the reporting BIS countries. While the Europe-based market has declined steadily in percentage terms, non-European centres favoured by tax, regulatory or regional considerations have shown above-average growth. Singapore, for example, has expanded from 1 per cent of the total in 1972 to 3 per cent in 1978, while the Bahamas/Grand Caymans represented 11 per cent in 1978 against 9 per cent in 1972.

One of the most significant aspects of the market's growth has been

TABLE A Estimated Size of Total Gross Euro-currency Market
(Amounts in $1000m, end-year)

	1972		1973		1974		1975		1976		1977		1978	
	Amount	% of Total	Amount	% of Total	Amount	% of Total	Amount	% of Total	Amount	% of Total	Amount	% of Total	Amount	% of Total
1. Euro-based Market														
Commercial Banks' External Assets	172	81	251	78	294	76	348	75	407	72	512	73	655	73
of which:														
Austria	NA	—	NA	—	NA	—	NA	—	NA	—	10	1	13	1
Belgium-Luxembourg	17	8	29	9	38	10	49	10	60	11	84	11	112	13
Denmark	NA	—	NA	—	NA	—	NA	—	NA	—	2	.3	3	.3
France	20	9	33	10	40	10	52	11	62	11	79	11	103	11
Germany	4	2	8	3	10	3	12	2	15	3	19	3	22	3
Ireland	NA	—	NA	—	NA	—	NA	—	NA	—	2	.3	2	.2
Italy	22	10	28	9	16	4	18	4	19	3	26	4	34	4
Netherlands	8	4	11	3	15	4	19	4	24	4	29	4	40	4
Sweden	1	1	2	1	2	1	3	1	3	1	3	1	4	.4
Switzerland	18	8	11	3	15	4	18	4	24	4	26	4	37	4
United Kingdom	83	39	128	40	158	41	178	39	202	36	231	33	287	32
2. Non-European Market:														
Bahamas & Grand Cayman	18	9	26	8	35	9	50	11	74	13	88	12	100	11
Bahrain	—	—	—	—	—	—	2	.4	6	1	16	2	23	3
Canada	8	4	12	4	14	4	14	3	17	3	18	3	22	3
Hong Kong	NA	—	4	1	7	2	9	2	15	2	17	2	21	2
Japan	10	5	17	5	21	5	20	4	22	4	22	3	34	4
Panama	1	1	2	1	5	1	6	1	8	1	10	1	13	1
Singapore	3	1	6	2	10	3	13	3	17	3	21	3	27	3
3. Grand Total Gross Market	212	100	319	100	386	100	462	100	565	100	704	100	897	100

Source: *Investors Chronicle*—21 September 1979—David Ashby
Note: Figures may not add due to rounding

the entry of new and existing banks into the various international financial centres. In November 1978, a total of 395 different financial institutions were represented in London either directly or through an equity interest in a London consortium bank; this figure includes 93 of the 100 largest banks in the world as measured by *The Banker*[5]. In terms of banks actually dealing in the Euro-currency market, a total of 254 banks as of November 1978 were authorised by the Bank of England to deal in foreign currencies and thereby participate in the Euro-market; as of January 1979, 348 banks were listed in Bank of England statistics on foreign currency activities of banks in the United Kingdom.[6] Table B provides as of January 1979 a breakdown of foreign currency assets and liabilities by category of bank in the London market.

The largest single component within the overall UK foreign currency market statistics is branches and subsidiaries of American banks, which reflects the importance of the dollar segment of the market and the relative priority given to international operations by these banks. While the American share of the London market has dropped from 50 per cent in 1970 to 38 per cent in mid-1975 and 33 per cent in early 1979, much of this decline reflects transfers of business to other branches for tax and administrative reasons. A total of 63 US banks in London in early 1979 thus had total sterling and foreign currency liabilities and capital funds in excess of the combined balance sheets of the UK clearing banks. In the period between 1975 and 1979, the market shares represented by Japanese and consortium banks remained at 14 per cent and 6 per cent respectively, while the category of 'other overseas banks' rose from 22 per cent to 28 per cent of the total.

Table B also points up the importance for London banks of overseas business; roughly two-thirds of their foreign currency liabilities and assets relate to non-UK residents. Japanese and consortium banks tend to have the highest concentration of assets in loans to overseas borrowers, with the UK clearing banks and accepting houses naturally lending a relatively high portion of assets to UK borrowers. Consortium banks—which include most Euro-banks—are by far the largest net takers from the London interbank market on a relative basis; 39 per cent of the former's foreign currency liabilities are derived from the interbank market while only 12 per cent of assets are re-lent to the market. Certificates of Deposit, which represent 10 per cent of total liabilities—with the US banks by far the largest issuers—total only 1 per cent of foreign currency assets of London banks. London banks as a whole in early 1979 were holding 20 per cent of their foreign currency assets in London interbank deposits, although the consortium

TABLE B *Breakdown of Foreign Currency Assets and Liabilities of UK Banks as of 17 January 1979 (amounts in £1000m.)*

	Assets		of which							
	Total Non-Sterling Assets		Loans to UK Banks		C/Ds		UK Borrowers		Overseas Borrowers	
	Amount	% of Total Banks	Amount	% of Total	Amount	% of Total	Amount	% of Total	Amount	% of Total
All Banks	139.6	100	27.7	20	1.6	1	11.2	8	98.9	71
of which:										
(a) London Clearing Banks	6.4	5	1.8	28	.7	11	1.5	23	3.0	47
(b) Accepting Houses	4.0	3	.8	20	.1	3	.5	13	2.5	63
(c) American Banks	46.0	33	7.8	17	.4	1	3.0	7	34.6	75
(d) Japanese Banks	19.4	14	3.3	17	—	—	1.1	6	14.9	77
(e) Consortium Banks	8.3	6	1.0	12	.1	1	.3	4	6.8	82
(f) Other Overseas Banks	38.9	28	10.0	26	.7	2	2.4	6	25.6	66

TABLE B (continued)

					Liabilities				
	Total Non-Sterling Liabilities		Deposits from UK Banking Sector		of which				
					Overseas Deposits		C/Ds	
	Amount	% of Total Banks	Amount	% of Total	Amount	% of Total	Amount	% of Total
All Banks	140.0	100	2.8	20	93.9	67	13.6	10
of which:								
(a) London Clearing Banks	6.3	5	1.3	21	4.0	64	.3	5
(b) Accepting Houses	4.1	3	1.2	29	2.5	1	.1	2
(c) American Banks	46.2	33	6.1	13	31.1	67	7.5	16
(d) Japanese Banks	19.6	14	4.3	22	12.6	64	2.4	12
(e) Consortium Banks	8.2	6	3.2	39	4.7	57	.1	1
(f) Other Overseas Banks	39.2	28	7.4	19	28.7	73	2.0	5

Source: Bank of England Quarterly Bulletin, vol. 19, no. 1 (March 1979).
Note: Total liabilities do not include small amounts of items in suspense, while total assets do not include small amounts of acceptances

category's share of 12 per cent was by far the lowest. Local UK customer business represented less than 7 per cent of total non-sterling assets for the categories of American, Japanese, consortium and other overseas banks.

The importance of London in terms of numbers of banks represented is shown by Table C, which provides a breakdown as of January 1979 in type of banking vehicle for thirty-two financial centres. With a total

TABLE C   *League Table of World Financial Centres–January 1979*

Country	Represen- tatives	Subsidiaries	Branches	Multi- national Affiliates	Total
London	83	62	209	71	425
New York	60	41	57	44	202
Hong Kong	64	66	43	26	199
Singapore	46	13	67	14	140
Tokyo	63	3	54	1	121
Sao Paulo	73	20	11	6	110
Nassau	–	32	61	5	98
Sydney	56	16	7	19	98
Frankfurt	49	10	24	5	88
Brussels	20	21	25	16	82
Mexico City	73	3	2	2	80
Jakarta	44	1	14	14	73
Luxembourg	–	47	8	16	71
Caracas	61	3	3	4	71
Zurich	19	30	17	4	70
Beirut	34	15	16	3	68
Los Angeles	15	16	17	19	67
Buenos Aires	43	4	17	2	66
Tehran	54	5	1	4	64
Geneva	6	28	8	10	52
Chicago	18	3	27	3	51
Madrid	41	5	3	2	51
Manila	14	4	17	9	51
San Francisco	5	14	13	13	45
Bogota	14	4	17	9	44
Melbourne	13	11	4	16	44
Panama	9	16	16	3	44
Rio de Janeiro	26	7	5	3	41
Milan	17	6	15	–	38
Bangkok	6	11	11	7	35
Johannesburg	19	8	3	3	33
Kuala Lumpur	7	1	7	7	22

Source: *Who is Where in World Banking* published by *The Banker* Research Unit

number of 425 vehicles ranging from representative offices to consortium banks, London has more than twice the number of vehicles as
New York with 202 and Hong Kong with 199. Within the overall
London total are 71 consortium affiliates and 62 subsidiaries, within
which categories are to be found the Euro-banks which are the focus of
this book. While London has retained its leadership as an operating base
for overseas banks, it should be noted that, in the period since
September 1975, the number of banking vehicles in London has actually
declined (from 449 to 425) while significant numerical growth has
occured in New York (179 to 202), Hong Kong (149 to 199) and
Singapore (111 to 140).

The Euro-bank which is the subject of this book does not represent a
significant share of the market in terms of collective or, with few
exceptions, individual size. While it is difficult—and not particularly
relevant—to quantify the importance of separately capitalised banks
which make up this category, a few unrelated numbers may be useful.
Consortium banks in London, which represent a major segment of the
Euro-bank sector, had total liabilities and capital in January 1979 of
£9,600 million, or 4 per cent of the UK banking sector total of £219,200
million.[7] At the close of their 1978 fiscal year, the forty consortium and
subsidiary banks in my statistical sample of London Euro-banks had
capital funds of £751 million and total assets of £12,624 million—
almost double the equivalent figures for fiscal 1974. London has
attracted by far the largest number of Euro-banks in large part because
of the size, sophistication and breadth of the interbank deposit market
which is essential to these relatively new banks as a source of deposits.
Other advantages include a flexible regulatory mechanism which has
proven forceful enough to restore calm during the 1974 crisis of
confidence, excellent communications, the attraction of London as a
residence for senior executives and the infrastructure and international
banking tradition which London has established over centuries as the
leading international financial centre.

While London has attracted the great majority of Euro-banks
because of the size and efficiency of its interbank and other markets, a
somewhat smaller number of these banks have set up operations in other
money centres. While an active interbank dealing market usually exists
in these centres and a certain amount of loan syndication takes place,
London generally is a substantial net provider of funds to both the
interbank and syndication markets in these other centres, particularly in
periods of credit stringency. Excluding tax haven centres such as the
Bahamas and Grand Caymans where some Euro-banks may be legally

incorporated with operating headquarters elsewhere, the sub-markets with a particularly large concentration of Euro-banks are Luxembourg, Singapore and Hong Kong. In each case, the amount of locally-oriented business done by Euro-banks is nominal or non-existent, as the choice of location has been based on the factors of cost, proximity to growing market areas, tax, flexibility of regulations, ease of entry, communications and difference in time zone.

Each of these and other centres offers different trade-offs to the stockholders of Euro-banks, and extensive feasibility studies generally precede the decision to open in one centre or another. For some of the largest American, British, Japanese and European banks, some form of participation in each major Euro-currency centre, often through a Euro-bank affiliate, is considered necessary, whereas smaller banks tend to concentrate their international overseas operations in a more limited number of locations.

The management issues faced by Euro-bankers in different financial centres must obviously be dealt with in the economic, regulatory and market context of their particular financial centre. Tax structure, ratio and other regulatory requirements imposed by local authorities, operating cost structure, the extent of and access to local currency business, time zone and other factors relating to communications, availability of trained staff, exchange controls, local political and economic conditions and other factors all have a significant impact on the management of Euro-banks in these centres. As discussed in subsequent chapters, however, the key Euro-bank management issues which are the subject of this book are not primarily a function of location so that the following paragraphs summarise only briefly the structure and factors which have led to the establishment of Euro-banks in centres outside the principal one of London.

Luxembourg, where a total of seventy-one banks, including forty-seven subsidiary banks and sixteen consortium institutions, had established themselves as of January 1979,[8] offers Euro-banks access to the Euro-market deposit and securities markets, a relatively attractive gearing ratio and operational features which have proven attractive to German and Scandinavian parents of Euro-banks. Most importantly, it has offered German banks a convenient locus for Euro-currency business which avoids such Bundesbank regulations as reserve requirements on international business which otherwise would exclude them from participation in the market. Twenty-seven Luxembourg banks are thus owned individually or collectively by German banks. In recent years, Scandinavian banks, which must use an overseas subsidiary to participate fully in the Euro-market, have opened Euro-banks in Luxembourg in preference to centres such as London. In addition, a number of other Luxembourg-based Euro-banks are owned by Belgian, North American and other European financial institutions attracted by cost, convenience, tax, linguistic and other factors.

The principal Euro-currency market in Asia is Singapore, which has sponsored the development since 1968 of the Asia-dollar market through a policy of selective entry into, and careful supervision of, the international money market there. Profiting from its central location in rapidly growing South Asia and its political stability as well as low tax and operating costs, the Singaporean government had granted licences by May 1979 to over 92 banks to deal in the Euro-currency (or Asia-dollar) market through Asian Currency Units (ACUs) which had total assets at end-1978 of $21.2 billion.[9] While most of this international deposit and lending activity is carried on by the branches of large international banks, in May 1979 there were 29 'merchant banks' generally owned by American, Japanese and European financial institutions, often with local partners who have set up wholly-owned or consortium subsidiaries on a regional basis to carry on an international investment and commercial banking business with emphasis on medium-term Euro-currency lending to Asian borrowers and participation in the Asian dollar bond market. Singapore's strength in the late 1970s as a market centre has been based on the breadth of the deposit and foreign exchange markets there, whereas the loan syndication market has tended to move to Hong Kong.

The other major Asian centre for Euro-banks is Hong Kong, which offers much the same advantages as Singapore as well as a more relaxed regulatory climate. While uncertainty with regard to the withholding tax on interest paid restrained the development of a money market competitive with that of Singapore, this tax has not prevented the syndication and booking of Euro-currency loans involving non-Hong Kong residents, and Hong Kong has developed into a loan and bond syndication centre along the lines of the London market. As of January 1979, a total of 92 subsidiaries and consortia had been set up, mostly since 1972, by North American, Japanese and European financial institutions on a wholly-owned or consortium basis to specialise in Asian-oriented investment and commercial banking business.[10]

Attracted by the importance of the French economy and financial markets, a number of Euro-banks have also been established in Paris despite the general concern on the part of foreign bankers with regard to what is often considered excessive control of their activities by the

Banque de France. Several of the older Euro-banks were opened in Paris, while more recent additions include Arab-oriented consortium banks with strong French sponsorship. In addition to these four markets, individual Euro-banks have been set up in recent years in Brussels, Beirut, Zurich, Geneva and other cities.

In mid-1979, a list of specific objectives for the Euro-banks in the London market might include one or more of the following:

(1) enable a commercial bank (particularly Japanese or American owned, in the context of Edge Act legislation) to diversify into investment banking activities such as underwriting, securities dealing and the taking of equity interests;

(2) earn a higher return on capital than the parent can in its traditional activities;

(3) place surplus funds generated by stockholder banks into the international interbank market and enable stockholders to participate in Euro-currency syndicated loans;

(4) enable banks with little international experience to become acquainted with the international deposit and lending market;

(5) serve in effect as an international branch in a specific financial centre for stockholder banks which are unable to establish one due to local or home country regulations;

(6) attract international funds to the country or region in which the stockholders are located or to the parent itself;

(7) serve as a common vehicle for a formal or informal grouping of individual banks with similar interests or objectives;

(8) represent the parent bank in a major international money market to expand its international network;

(9) extend the range of international services provided the parents' domestic customers, in particular if competitor banks already have a significant Euro-market base;

(10) serve as a marketing vehicle for the syndicated loans generated by the network of a large parent bank;

(11) serve as a focal point for a number of international banks interested in doing business in a particular country or region;

(12) enable a non-banking institution to participate in the Euro-currency market; and

(13) enable stockholders to participate in the medium-term Euro-currency lending market in general or in a specific type of lending such as shipping or energy finance.

The stockholder ties among consortium banks extend from purely *ad hoc* arrangements built around that consortium venture to a closely integrated group which co-operates in other sectors as well. In certain instances the Euro-bank acts as a direct extension of the parents' activities which may severely restrict the areas of activity open to the Euro-bank, whereas in others a more opportunistic approach is taken with the ultimate object to maximise profitability. A number of large international banks have participated in the formation of a variety of Euro-banks throughout the world, while others have expanded only through their branch networks or a limited number of specialised or wholly-owned subsidiaries.

A number of Euro-bank ownership patterns have evolved over the past decade. First, the wholly-owned subsidiary is usually established by a relatively large national bank to provide a particular service or fill a specific gap in the parent's geographic network which another corporate entity cannot. Such subsidiaries may act as the Euro-currency loan syndicating arm of a large US money centre bank, operate in financial markets where the parent cannot legally open a branch, perform an underwriting function which would be illegal in a different corporate form or simply provide a more flexible management environment than would be the case for a branch.

A second ownership pattern is that of the majority-controlled subsidiary with a limited number of minority partners. The corporate objectives of such a bank may be similar to that of the wholly-owned subsidiary – to conduct specialist activities or operate in a limited geographic market – but minority shareholders have been brought in to provide a local partner, specialist expertise or other requirements to achieve stated objectives. Local partners are an obvious choice for a foreign bank entering a new market and may even represent a prerequisite for entry by local authorities, while other minority stock-holders may provide a source of funds or new business contacts as well as market experience.

A broad ownership range with no single dominant stockholder represents the third ownership pattern. In some of these cases, a single bank – often a London merchant bank – has taken the initiative of bringing together into a single consortium a relatively large number of foreign banks who may be characterised by their lack of international financial expertise, interest in becoming involved in a particular geographic or functional sector of the Euro-currency market or common background – such as ownership by savings or co-operative banks. Many of the earlier consortium banks were established on the basis of historically strong personal or business ties among banks from a variety of countries who felt that a minority stake in a consortium bank was the best approach to the rapidly growing Euro-currency market. A trend in the late 1960s towards the formation of international banking 'clubs' of banks committed to work together internationally without a legal merger, resulted in the formation of a number of consortia designed to embody this co-operative commitment.

Single country or regional consortia are composed of banks from a given country or region who come together to pool their resources in a venture they would not undertake individually because of limited financial or personnel resources; in the case of countries such as Japan, such a pooling of resources may have been a prerequisite to receiving official approval to establish an overseas entity, while several Scandinavian groupings have been set up on the basis of historical ties among the Nordic countries. A different type of multi-bank regional consortium is one whose marketing objectives rather than ownership pattern relate to a particular country or region. Such banks bring together a variety of international banks often chosen to provide the widest possible geographic representation, and one or more banks from a specific country or region such as Eastern Europe, Latin America or the Arab countries to develop business specifically in that country or region.

A full range of possible Euro-bank activities would include the following:

(1) taking of call, short date and fixed date Euro-currency deposits of up to several years from the interbank market and customers to fund the bank's own loan portfolio and for relending in the interbank market;

(2) exchange dealing in spot and forward Euro-currencies and often the local currency of the stockholder for the account of clients, the bank's own position or to create deposits through the swap;

(3) Euro-currency lending for the bank's own book on a rollover or fixed rate basis from short dates to medium-term (the latter having exceeded ten years at various times in recent years) to governments and government agencies, corporations and individuals throughout the world on a secured or unsecured basis. Often lending activity in the local currency of the market in which the bank is located represents a significant portion of the portfolio;

(4) management of Euro-currency rollover loans on an underwriting or best efforts basis to be placed with the stockholder group or a wider range of banks;

(5) origination, management, underwriting and selling of publicly issued Euro-bonds and Euro-equities; provision of a secondary trading market in Euro-bonds;
(6) arrangement of private placements of fixed-rate debt issues in a variety of currencies with international investors;
(7) corporate finance activities such as project structuring, corporate restructuring and mergers and acquisitions;
(8) provision of traditional trade finance or correspondent banking services through the opening of letters of credit, acceptance finance, money transfer and collection;
(9) portfolio management for international investors;
(10) arrangement of lease finance either with or without the use of a tax shield;
(11) arrangement of export finance through one or more national export credit agencies;
(12) the taking of equity participations either on an outright basis or in connection with the extension of a loan;
(13) specialist project financing capability in sectors such as energy and shipping.

Few Euro-banks are active in all these sectors, and many limit themselves for practical purposes to Euro-currency lending and the deposit and exchange dealing necessary to support this activity. Certain banks, which are often described as merchant banks, emphasise fee generation through the origination and syndication of Euro-loans and Euro-bonds, whereas at the other extreme some banks derive earnings primarily through interest differential income on Euro-currency loans taken from other banks. The latter banks usually possess a relatively large capital base compared with that of the investment banking or fee-oriented institutions. Net stockholder funds including subordinated debt for the sample of forty banks ranged from £4 million to £97 million at the end of fiscal 1978.

The management of most Euro-banks is usually characterised by a higher degree of autonomy than would exist in the home office or a direct branch of a parent shareholder. Justified by such factors as the different nature of the subsidiary's activity, time and geographic distance, and the express desire of the stockholders to create a more flexible and opportunistic vehicle than the parent, this relative autonomy can be significantly restricted in the event of poor operating results of the Euro-bank or the advent of a cautious lending or investing policy on the part of the parents. Senior management of a Euro-bank is usually either seconded from a stockholder bank or recruited from one of the major international commercial banks, an investment or merchant bank or another Euro-bank.

In many cases an experienced, mature chief executive is chosen from one of the British clearing banks or similar institutions on the basis of his relatively conservative approach to his responsibilities, whereas in other situations a relatively young man is attracted to the position on the basis of its relative autonomy and compensation, which may include an incentive element.

Given the dual investment and commercial banking objectives of many Euro-banks and the relatively small number of qualified individuals with experience in both sectors, locating appropriate senior management has not been an easy task for Euro-bank sponsors. In view of the importance of interest differential income, their familiarity with these activities and the relative ease of generating this type of income, many stockholder banks have engaged individuals with essentially commercial banking backgrounds after unsuccessful attempts to locate the ideal individual with experience in both commercial and investment banking.

Entry into the London market for a new Euro-bank has not been difficult for a bank with backing from established financial institutions. The British authorities have welcomed new entrants to an international market centre which they have deliberately freed from restrictions imposed by other national authorities, and the principal barrier to entry is authorisation by the Bank of England to deal in foreign exchange and foreign currency deposits. In recent years, such approval has been granted following a relatively brief trial period to the Euro-bank affiliates of foreign banking institutions of a size and stature the Bank considers adequate to provide sufficient support to the London affiliate. No minimum capital guidelines have been established, although in recent years most new Euro-banks have opened up with an initial paid-in capital of at least several million pounds. The Bank also vets the qualifications and reputation of senior management, in particular those of the senior money manager of the new bank.

The UK regulatory climate in which the London-based Euro-bank operates involves a minimum of specific guidelines and an emphasis on flexible, personal, evolving and participative supervision.[11] Euro-banks are regulated in the sterling market and have been subject to corset-type lending restrictions. Euro-currency business which does not involve UK residents or sterling transactions is effectively unregulated, and since the sterling business of most Euro-banks is a small fraction of their total activity, these banks achieve a freedom of operation which is fairly unique in a major money centre.

Following the secondary banking crisis of 1973–4, a statutory framework has evolved in the late 1970s under which a two-tiered system of recognised banks and licensed deposit-taking institutions was established in 1979 under the Bank of England's supervision. Only the former, which will include most of the present authorised banks and those carrying on a Euro-banking activity, will be permitted to use the word 'bank' in their trade name. This more structured approach to regulation has been accompanied by a more intensive and sophisticated effort to determine a bank's capital adequacy by focusing on the level of overall gearing and classification of risk assets. The Bank of England has informed Euro-banks, for example, that it regards a gearing range of 15–20:1 to be appropriate for such institutions carrying on a Euro-currency lending activity and that a higher level of gearing must be justified to their satisfaction. In addition, a capital adequacy formula weighting each category of assets by presumed level of risk is being evolved.

In contrast to the extensive ratio and credit controls applied to banks established in other major financial centers, the only numerical ratio guideline applied to banks established in the UK in mid-1979 is the minimum reserve ratio applied to sterling deposits for purposes of monetary policy control. As of mid-1979 this required that a minimum of $12\frac{1}{2}$ per cent of sterling deposit liabilities not used to finance sterling interbank assets be held in such reserve assets as cash at the Bank of England, money at call in the London Discount Market and certain government securities. In the event, Euro-banks have generally maintained ratios significantly in excess of this minimum. Selective and general controls on sterling lending have been imposed from time to time in the past, and in mid-1979 a 'corset' control on the growth of interest-bearing sterling liabilities was in effect.

The Euro-banks discussed in the following chapters are primarily UK-incorporated banks owned by foreign stockholders, although there have been included a few branches of foreign Euro-banks which derive a significant portion of their earnings from their London branch. Operating generally from a single office in the City of London, these banks usually are organised along functional lines with separate money market/Euro-bond, lending, credit, administrative and corporate finance departments reporting to a chief executive. The size of staff is a function of the bank's overall volume of business, the extent of personnel-intensive functions such as documentary credit or bond dealing operations, the relative importance of services to be provided stockholders or clients, and the extent of business development and loan syndication activities carried on by the Euro-bank. The London-based Euro-banks in the sample shown in Appendix 1 had staff levels ranging from 14 to 260 with an average of 85.[12] For the thirty-eight Euro-banks which indicated staff as well as asset levels at the time, the amount of assets per employee extended from a low of £.6 million to a high of £15.3 million with an average of £4.5 million. The highest asset/employee figures were shown by Euro-banks whose principal activity lies in taking participations in medium-term Euro-currency loans and funding these loans, with the lowest ratios indicated by banks with major loan generation and syndication as well as Euro-bond activities.

London-based Euro-banks often have established overseas branches, affiliates and representative offices. Euro-bank officers may be posted to the parent bank's country as well as major overseas market areas such as the Pacific Basin, Latin America or the Arab Gulf for business development purposes. Participations are taken in Euro-banks, often affiliated with the stockholder groups, in other market centres; quite often the London-based Euro-bank acts as the coordinating vehicle for the world-wide investment banking network of a large international bank or informal 'club' of such banks. Investments are made by Euro-banks in London or overseas-based non-banking institutions such as financial service, leasing and venture capital companies to provide a broader range of customer services.

Smaller samples of eight banks each have been taken from Euro-banks based in Hong Kong, Singapore and Luxembourg. The smaller sample size essentially reflects the relatively limited number of Euro-banks in these markets which have an identity separate from that of the parent institution. In the former two instances, the structure and activities of the sample banks generally resemble those of the London sample with an emphasis on regional business derived from the Asian market, although in some cases Euro-banks functioning in large part as a branch substitute have been included to provide a meaningful sample size. In the case of Luxembourg, virtually all of the sample banks function largely as a proxy for branches, but the requirement of a separate capitalisation and the local regulatory approach to these banks as self-standing institutions justify inclusion of these institutions as Euro-banks at least for purposes of comparison with banks in London, Singapore and Hong Kong.

Such factors as wide differentials in effective tax rates as well as different regulatory guidelines with respect to gearing and other ratios obviously limit the analytical conclusions which can be drawn from a comparison between Euro-banks in the four different financial centres. On balance, however, management behaviour in all of these centres reflects the challenges and problems of building a young institution in an increasingly competitive, mature and global Euro-currency market. While local structural considerations thus frame an individual Euro-bank's performance, over a reasonable period of time the relative profitability of Euro-banks in each of these centres ultimately reflects such factors as management competence and stockholder contribution.

The chapters which follow provide a detailed analysis of Euro-bank asset management (Chapter 3), liability management (Chapter 4), other income-producing activities (Chapter 5), and an analysis of Euro-bank profitability (Chapter 6). The chapters are based in large part on my own personal experience and observations from eleven years in the Euro-markets, but to provide a broader and more representative spectrum of experience a total of forty in-depth interviews have been held with the senior management, in most cases the chief executive, of Euro-banks whose principal base of activity and source of revenue is the London market.

One possible weakness of the sample interviews is that too much emphasis might be placed on current management policies in response to contemporary market conditions and problems, as opposed to strategies dealing with fundamental management issues. By emphasising the latter in our discussions, however, and placing these conversations in the context of a longer-term personal involvement in the Euro-currency market, I hope I have effectively dealt with this issue. Appendix 1 lists the banks included in the statistical sample, which, in the case of the London institutions, contains all but two of the banks interviewed.

The original London interviews were conducted in mid-1975. Four years later, in connection with the publication of the second edition of this book, virtually all of the banks in the original sample were interviewed again with the primary intent of determining what significant changes, if any, had occurred in management policies and practices in the intervening period. In view of the large number of structural changes which had taken place—in almost two—thirds of the sample either the chief executive had changed and/or a significant stockholder restructuring had taken place—these up-dates provided a very useful insight into the evolution of Euro-bank policy in the late 1970s.

APPENDIX 1   Composition of Statistical Sample

Bank	Date Established	Total Assets at end-1978	Total Stock-holder Funds at end-1978
		(amounts in mm.)	
A – LONDON BANKS			
Banque Belge Ltd	1934	260.7	£14.3
Midland and International Banks Ltd	1964	£976.6	£47.1
Dow Banking Corporation	1965	SF1570.7	SF167.0
United Bank of Kuwait	1966	£396.4	£14.3
International Commercial Bank Ltd	1967	£505.7	£31.6
Amex Bank Ltd (a)	1967	£346.7	£21.0
Allied Bank International	1968	$756.8	$45.9
Banque Francaise de Credit Internationale (b)	1968	£80.1	£5.3
Manufacturers Hanover Ltd	1968	£175.8	£10.7
Bank of Tokyo and Detroit Ltd (c)	1968	£175.5	£11.7
Atlantic International Bank Ltd	1969	£135.1	£7.5
Bankers Trust International Ltd (d)	1969	£73.6	£9.5
Scandinavian Bank Ltd	1969	£1026.3	£33.4
Associated Japanese Bank Ltd	1970	£458.6	£24.8
Japan International Bank Ltd	1970	£383.3	£20.0
Chemical Bank International Ltd	1970	£108.9	£6.9
Orion Bank Ltd	1970	£1115.3	£54.3
United International Bank Ltd	1970	£239.8	£12.7
Bank of America International Ltd	1971	£264.2	£16.6
Marine Midland Bank Ltd	1971	£86.1	£9.6
London Interstate Bank Ltd	1971	£85.9	£6.9
Nordic Bank Ltd	1971	£1069.1	£96.6
Credit Suisse White Weld Ltd (d) (e)	1971	£72.2	£11.1
Continental Illinois Ltd	1972	£202.9	£10.6
European Brazilian Bank Ltd	1972	£386.8	£22.1

APPENDIX 1	*(continued)*

Bank	Date Established	Total Assets at end-1978	Total Stock-holder Funds at end-1978
		(amounts in mm.)	
Italian International Bank Ltd	1972	£165.2	£12.8
Libra Bank Ltd	1972	£449.4	£22.6
Merrill Lynch International Bank Ltd	1972	£174.5	£8.5
UBAF Ltd	1972	£471.9	£18.9
Wells Fargo Ltd	1972	£139.6	£8.5
Anglo Romanian Bank Ltd	1973	£122.2	£4.9
Banco Urquijo Hispano Americano Ltd	1973	£103.9	£6.4
European Banking Co. Ltd	1973	£308.7	£19.0
First International Bancshares Ltd (*f*)	1973	£132.3	£10.0
Hungarian International Bank Ltd	1973	£112.6	£6.2
International Energy Bank Ltd	1973	£224.1	£13.1
Iran Overseas Bank Ltd	1973	£150.2	£10.0
London and Continental Bankers Ltd	1973	£267.7	£18.0
Bank Brussels Lambert Ltd	1974	£112.3	£4.3
International Mexican Bank Ltd	1974	$442.7	$33.0

B – SINGAPORE BANKS   (in mm. of Singapore $)

Bank		Total Assets at end-1978	Total Stock-holder Funds at end-1978
Singapore International Merchant Bank Ltd		108.7	10.6
Asian American Merchant Bank Ltd		96.3	12.2
Temenggong Merchant Bankers Ltd		18.6	3.6
United Chase Merchant Bankers Ltd		165.1	15.0
Dresdner (South East Asia) Ltd		873.4	39.4
DBS–Daiwa Securities International Ltd		121.4	6.8
Singapore–Japan Merchant Bank Ltd		NA	NA
Morgan Guaranty Pacific Ltd		171.3	12.7

APPENDIX 1   *(continued)*

Bank	Date Established	Total Assets at end-1978	Total Stock-holder Funds at end-1978
		(amounts in mm.)	
C – HONG KONG BANKS		(in US$mm. unless otherwise noted)	
Trident International Finance Ltd		HK$609.6 mm	HK$68.6 mm
First National Boston (HK) Ltd		113.1	7.0
Baring Brothers Asia Ltd		121.7	17.8
Wardley Limited		611.8	35.5
Orion Pacific Ltd		148.9	11.3
IBJ Finance		HK$1724.7	HK$126.6
WestLB Asia Ltd		HK$1195	HK$121.9
D – LUXEMBOURG BANKS		(in—mm. of Lux. Francs unless otherwise noted)	
(capital funds figure excludes provisions for contingencies and depreciation)			
Canadian American Bank SA		US$204.3 mm	US$12.0 mm
WestLB International		108.4	3.5
Bayerische Vereinsbank International		64.9	1.6
Commerzbank International		177.6	5.1
BFG Luxembourg		79.6	3.0
Christiania Bank og Kredit-kasse International SA		91	.4
PKBanken International (Luxembourg)		17.9	.4
Compagnie Luxembourgeoise de la Dresdner Bank AG		221.7	5.1

Note: year-end approximately 31 December 1978. For banks with fiscal years ending up to and including 30 June 1979 latest figures available at the time of writing have been used.
(a) formerly Rothschild Intercontinental Bank Ltd
(b) formerly Brown Harriman International Bank Ltd
(c) formerly Western American Bank (Europe) Ltd; now Bank of Tokyo International Ltd
(d) banks originally established at earlier date but began significant Euro-currency operations in year indicated
(e) now Credit Suisse First Boston Ltd
(f) now First Dallas Ltd

3 Asset Management

Asset management is one of the Euro-bank chief executive's highest priorities in view of the importance usually placed by stockholders on participation in the medium-term Euro-currency deposit and lending market and the relative facility with which a loan portfolio can be built up to earn a return on invested capital. While many Euro-banks – particularly subsidiaries of the large American commercial banks – as a matter of policy do not carry a significant loan portfolio on their own books, interest differential income and fees derived from loan participations represent the dominant source of income for most Euro-banks.

While no officially published data covers the exact market segment represented by my definition of Euro-bank, Bank of England statistics on 'consortium banks', which represent the bulk of London Euro-bank assets, provide a useful indication of the asset breakdown for the typical London–based Euro-bank. Table D provides a detailed breakdown of

TABLE D   *Asset Composition* of London Consortium Banks*
(amounts in £mm)

| | As of 16 July 1975 | | As of 17 January 1979 | |
	Amount	% of Total	Amount	% of Total
Reserve Assets	43	.8	44	.5
Special Deposits	8	.1	8	.1
Deposits with UK Banks + Discount Market	1089	19.9	1301	13.4
Certificates of Deposit	269	4.9	232	2.4
Loans to UK Borrowers	665	12.1	791	8.2
Other Loans and Bills	3298	60.1	6977	72.1
Investments	69	1.3	167	1.7
Other Assets (including acceptances, etc.)	44	.8	152	1.6
Total	5485	100.0	9672	100.0

Source: *Bank of England Quarterly Bulletin* vol. 19 no. 1 (March 1979)

* Sterling plus foreign currency

consortium bank assets as of 16 July 1975, when the data were first published, and as of 17th January, 1979.

Over 80 per cent of consortium bank assets in early 1979 were represented by customer loans, principally to overseas borrowers in Euro-currencies, with the bulk of the remainder applied to interbank deposits and certificates of deposit. The comparable 1975 figure for customer loans was 72 per cent. The decrease in liquid, low-yielding assets reflects the growing maturity of these banks and the pressure to increase earnings. Sterling assets as of January 1979 accounted for only 12 per cent of total assets, a slight drop from 15 per cent in 1975. With the exception of several wholly-owned Euro-bank subsidiaries of US banks, the asset composition of non-consortium London Euro-banks should not differ significantly from the figures in Table D. Among the smaller asset categories, reserve assets accounted for less than 1 per cent of total assets; as of January 1979, the consortium bank reserve asset ratio was 19.7 per cent, significantly in excess of the $12\frac{1}{2}$ per cent minimum requirement. Investments of 1.7 per cent of assets represent primarily holdings of UK government securities and Euro-bonds.

For day-to-day liquidity purposes, Euro-banks rely on prime bank certificates of deposits as well as money at call in the discount market, short-term loans to other banks and possibly a short date gilt portfolio. While during the early 1970s a wide variety of London banks issued dollar and sterling certificates of deposit, during the 1974 crisis of confidence following the Franklin and Herstatt failures, the market for all but the most prime names – generally the top ten US banks and British clearing banks – dried up to the extent that banks looking for liquidity in their certificate of deposit portfolio felt obliged to concentrate on these prime names.

The two principal asset categories are loans to other banks and customer loans. The ratio between these two, which is one of the few which is usually revealed in published data and considered relevant by the management of some Euro-banks, is a matter of debate both as to its significance as well as to the appropriate ratio. Loans to other banks, which are made for periods of up to one year and in some cases longer, generally provide a minimal return to the lending bank if matched by a corresponding deposit. The $\frac{1}{8}$ per cent spread between the quoted bid and asked rates in the London interbank market provides a theoretical indication of the interest margin available on such loans. In practice, particularly during periods of market nervousness, Euro-banks are rarely among those institutions able to take funds at the bid rate, and when the tiering of the interbank market in the form of offered rates quoted as a function of a borrower's presumed creditworthiness followed the 1974 crisis, they often found themselves paying the offered rate or even higher.

While it is therefore possible to make a marginal spread on an interbank loan by lending on a matched basis to another bank which pays more for its money than the lending institution, the presumed credit risk and low yield involved limits the extent of this business. In practice, interbank lending on a matched basis for many Euro-banks involves a breakeven or marginal profit or loss operation with the level of profitability often a function of the quality of the banks to whom funds are lent.

In view of this profit constraint, the extent of most Euro-banks' lending to other banks is a function of the desired level of liquidity, published balance sheet ratios, the need to maximise profits and the importance of being seen by other banks to be both a lender as well as a taker of interbank funds. While fixed-term loans to other banks presumably involve a minimal level of risk, breaking such a deposit for liquidity purposes would be considered one of the last ditches of defence in a crisis. As for the appropriate ratio for balance sheet purposes, most Euro-bankers agree that there is no ideal relationship between interbank loans and other assets in view of the great differences among banks in terms of leverage, quality of assets and business objectives. Those bankers that have a specific relationship in mind usually think in terms of a fifty-fifty ratio between interbank and customer loans, with a few others aiming at a smaller portion of interbank loans. Bankers interviewed in 1979 indicated that very few changes had taken place since 1975 in their views of the appropriate ratios.

As a result, the principal objective of Euro-banks in maintaining a given amount of interbank loans is to be seen to be operating on both sides of the interbank market. While it is universally recognised that Euro-banks are generally net takers of interbank funds, a bank feels that being able to make a two-way quote to other banks reflects favourably both on its credit rating and its professionalism. In times of market stress and nervousness, making such a two-way market for practical purposes may involve lending out short date (up to one week in maturity) rather than fixed date (from one week to one year) funds both because of liquidity objectives and the relative unavailability of longer date deposits.

The management of the customer loan portfolio is often regarded by the chief executive as his principal priority. The implicit priority traditionally given by bankers to loan quality is reinforced among Euro-bankers by their institutions' relative newness to the market and corresponding relative lack of substantial retained earnings to meet potential losses. The normal sense of professionalism in terms of one's loss record is thus heightened by the practical knowledge that one's profitability if not viability as well as the path of one's career are vitally dependent on minimising loan losses. On the other hand, the easy availability of loan participations through the syndication process and the historically almost unique phenomenon of starting a new business with a large capital base but no loans, created strong pressures to build up a large loan portfolio in a short period of time. Throughout history new banks have usually built up their base of stockholder funds through retained earnings from the gradual and profitable build-up of assets and new capital which is attracted by this profitable growth. On the contrary, the typical Euro-banker on opening for business often finds himself with a paid-in capital of at least several million pounds, a substantial overhead to amortise and the implicit or spoken requirement to meet certain earnings targets which in reality can only be met in the short term by putting loans on the books. To these powerful incentives is added the natural human desire of the chief executive to produce an earnings record and build a significant asset base.

Torn by these conflicting pressures, the Euro-banker responds by building a loan portfolio which in his mind best balances the objectives of minimal individual credit risk, building customer relationships, diversification of risk, attractive profitability, shortest maturity and any other specific objectives established by the stockholders. The latter may relate to geographic or industry specialisation, maturity, the relative importance of own-generated business and other factors.

Individual credit risk, the evaluation of which is usually viewed by the banker as his professional stock in trade, also poses some of the most difficult problems in view of the nature of today's Euro-currency market. Historically, loss experience in international lending has been extremely low. A comparison of the international loss record of seven major US banks for the period 1971–7, for example, indicates that such write-offs have remained well below those incurred on domestic lending.[1] It can be argued, however, that this excellent experience was a function of an unchecked boom in world trade and investment; that most international business was done in the 1950s and 1960s with prime multinational companies who have rarely failed to meet their own and their subsidiaries' obligations, and that the business was being carried on primarily by large American and European commercial banks with significant international lending experience.

On the other hand, Euro-banks are much more dependent on business taken from the syndication market, which at least implies that the very best business from a credit standpoint may be held in portfolio by the syndicating banks rather than sold to the market. It is quite apparent, for example, that short term finance for their corporate customers, which traditionally has been the backbone of international banking, is generally kept within the portfolio of major international banks, and Euro-banks usually participate in the business only if it is channeled to them by a parent bank. More importantly, the nature of Euro-currency lending has shifted markedly during the 1970s towards longer maturities, a greater involvement in finance for large projects with a significant commodity, technological or competitive risk; and a much larger component of country risk, in particular countries which do not have a long or positive record of borrowing from the private banking sector. In 1978, for example, borrowers from a total of eighty-three different countries were shown in publicised credits listed by the International Bank for Reconstruction and Development; in the active year of 1974, the corresponding figure was only sixty-two. In mid-1979, the effective continuing defaults of sovereign borrowers such as Turkey and Zaire had begun to qualify the optimism of bankers who had previously maintained that such borrowers could not afford to default.

Faced with these constraints and the obvious difficulty in evaluating so many of the credits available to him, the Euro-banker may respond in several ways to the challenge of risk control. One alternative is to opt for 'name' credits which are generally accepted in the marketplace and/or by the stockholders as involving at worst only a nominal risk and not necessitating any original credit work. While what constitutes an acceptable 'name' may change over time, major Western governments and their agencies and prime multinational corporations generally fall into this category. In such cases, the principal decision variables are pricing, amount, maturity and possibly reciprocity. The implicit assumption in accepting such risks is often the apocalyptic argument to the effect that 'if X borrower defaults, then none of us will be around anyway to worry about collecting our principal'.

Another option is to rely on the parent bank or banks' credit judgement, which not only brings to bear the worldwide resources and credit information capabilities of a major international bank but also serves to shift responsibility from the Euro-bank executive to his stockholder in the event of future problems. Euro-bankers often admit to ignorance of a specific country but are prepared to participate in a credit because a stockholder is 'happy with the risk'. In a typical Euro-bank's control procedure, the extremely difficult question of country risk exposure is a matter of periodic dialogue with Board members who presumably bring to bear the particular expertise of their own institutions to set and revise country limits with the result that level of country risk is usually a shared decision. In many cases, the Euro-bank's country exposure is computed within the parent bank or banks' overall exposure to a given country or classification of countries, and a continual dialogue between management and stockholders revolves around the former's share of this global quota.

A third response is that of making independent judgements on the basis of the Euro-bank's own credit expertise. While most if not all Euro-banks have a separate credit department, in many instances this function is primarily an administrative one concerned with the mechanical spreading of statements, analysis of data and monitoring of existing loans, rather than an independent source of lending judgement. In making most credit decisions, reliance is usually placed by the chief executive on his own credit judgement or that of a few very experienced colleagues. In many cases Euro-banks have developed specialised expertise in industrial sectors such as shipping, real estate or energy financing or in certain geographic areas which is the province of key individuals in the bank's management or that of its stockholders; other banks often rely heavily on this specialist knowledge in taking participations in loans to sectors in which they have no direct experience. To the extent which their human resources and decision-making autonomy permit, individual Euro-banks form an independent judgement on individual country, sectoral and corporate risks through extensive travel, independent financial analysis of corporate borrowers and maintenance of contacts with a given industry.

Diversification of risk is one of the few variables in the management of the loan portfolio which can be controlled directly by the chief executive. Depending on the individual management's philosophy, a variety of control systems may be employed. Most banks have a maximum limit on exposure to one borrower or a related group of borrowers which generally ranges between 10–20 per cent of stockholders' funds. For banks with a relatively low absolute capital, the percentage may be a bit higher to enable them to take a $1 million participation in a given syndication. For banks which recognise a maximum exposure limit, there is often a distinction made by maturity (i.e. a higher percentage of net worth for short term loans) and by country (i.e. – a highly favoured government merits a higher percentage exposure). Over time, absolute single-borrower limits are usually increased as the bank's capital is augmented, although many have retained unchanged limits despite increases in net worth.

On the other hand, a number of banks maintain a large degree of flexibility in this respect. One category of these banks is comprised of Euro-banks with a specific vocation which emphasises the attracting of funds to a specific country or group of countries such as the Socialist bloc or Latin America. Placing a limit on exposure to the sole borrower in a Socialist country which sponsors that particular Euro-bank is naturally regarded as self-defeating. Another category is comprised of wholly-owned and consortium banks who regard themselves as an extension of their stockholders and therefore able to rely on the latters' resources. For a borrower who is a highly valued customer of one of the stockholders, several Euro-banks are prepared to lend up to and beyond their capital base with implicit support both as to credit and possible balance sheet assistance from a parent.

Country risk control represents another variable in the diversification of risk. Virtually all Euro-banks recognise that any absolute limit established is a highly judgemental and subjective decision, although a number of banks or their parents perform laborious analytical exercises by which individual countries' economic statistics are examined and different factors determining a country's ability and willingness to provide foreign exchange to meet its debts are analysed and weighted. Among the factors given significant consideration is a forward analysis of debt servicing capability as measured by dividing foreign currency debt service by projected exports and invisible income. Most bankers recognise that even this calculation must be refined significantly by judgemental factors; witness the fact that throughout the late 1970s, these ratios for such relatively popular borrowers as Mexico and Brazil were a significant multiple of those for Portugal and other less popular countries, while similar data for the highly regarded Socialist countries are simply not available.

Bankers interviewed in mid-1979 noted that the principal change in their approach to country risk since 1975 was a much greater refinement and formalisation of the process of fixing such limits. In the past, limits had often not been set formally or established without significant research on the basis of a specific lending opportunity or the influence of a key individual in the organisation. To the extent that any formula approach is applied to country risk, a limitation based on the Euro-bank's capital or percentage of loans outstanding seems to be most prevalent. Such a percentage, which might be 10 per cent of one's total portfolio or 50–100 per cent of one's net worth, is usually applied to less developed or other countries outside those represented by the stockholder groups, in which countries presumably such risks are acceptable or actually desirable from a strategic standpoint. A typical approach will be to place sovereign borrowers in several categories representing different percentages of the bank's net worth; countries represented by the stockholders or perceived as bearing no risk fall into an unlimited category, while lesser names fall into categories representing 100 per cent of net worth, 50 per cent and so forth.

In practice, given the regional preferences of banks set up to specialise in Latin America, the Arab world, Asia or the Socialist bloc, Euro-banks sponsored in such a fashion often have a preponderant proportion of their portfolio so allocated, and the risk of loss arising from such lack of geographic diversification is regarded by the chief executive as relating to the strength of the stockholder banks rather than his own balance sheet. While country risk control is thus given an apparent high priority by management, its limitations for the reasons given above are usually frankly admitted by management. One consortium bank executive who has a highly refined country risk control system pointed out that his only potential loan losses to date were located in the US and UK, the only countries for which limits had not been established because of the presumed absence of country risk. Bankers also admitted to the flexibility of country limits in the event of a change in economic or political climate, the appearance of an interesting piece of business or another opportunistic factor. Bankers also recognise that modifying a country limit upon receipt of unfavourable news does not eliminate an existing exposure which may still have several years to run, while there is some intellectual inconsistency in changing basic lending policy in response to short term developments such as the decision by stockholder banks' official examiners to classify a given type of risk, unexpected political events and episodic occurrences such as the discovery of oil.

Other limits placed for purposes of diversification of risk usually relate to exposure to industries or sectors which are perceived to carry a certain risk in aggregate. These limitations have been placed in recent years on sectors borrowing heavily from the Euro-currency market such as shipping, real estate and the petroleum industry which often happen to be the specialist preserve of a number of Euro-banks. In practice, however, these limits have a discontinuous or *ex post* characteristic in the sense that no further exposure to such a sector is permitted if internal analysis or market sentiment results in a negative management attitude toward the sector.

Very little official data on the composition of Euro-bank loan portfolios has been published, and individual banks have been reluctant to divulge even the broader industrial or geographic categories making up their portfolios. Of some assistance in evaluating such portfolios in general, however, is Bank for International Settlements data on the gross and net exposure of international banks to individual countries. While the data base given in Table E does not include all banks with overseas exposures, it is sufficiently complete to enable the analyst to draw some tentative conclusions. The individual countries in the table include most of the larger net borrowers, although certain countries have been excluded as they represent either intermediate financial centres (Hong Kong, Bahamas) or countries of incorporation where the true risk probably lies elsewhere (Panama, Liberia).

From Table E can be seen the wide geographic distribution of the overall loan portfolio of the international banking sector. Even such heavy borrowers as Brazil and Mexico represent only 3.5 per cent and 2.6 per cent, respectively, of gross bank claims. While such diversification of risk is true for the system as a whole, however, individual banks may diverge sharply from the norm. Another conclusion to be drawn from the data is that the system's proportionate exposure is relatively low to countries where a significant perceived credit exists. The heaviest borrowers, Germany and Japan, have absolutely prime credit ratings, while even those at the other end of the credit spectrum—say, Algeria, Peru, Turkey and Yugoslavia—each represent well below 1 per cent of the system's gross exposure. Once again, however, the analyst must look at the exposure of individual banks to draw any valid conclusions at the microeconomic level.

A third variable used to control a Euro-bank portfolio is maturity as measured either by average life or ultimate maturity. Average life is computed by dividing the total principal amount of a loan into the sum of each principal repayment multiplied by the period of time it is outstanding.

Maturity is relevant both in terms of credit exposure and profitability in view of the market practice of fixing the interest spread throughout the life of a loan regardless of intervening changes in credit rating or market conditions. The relevance of variations in maturity is pointed up by Table F, which traces the pattern of final maturity period for five regular sovereign borrowers on the Euro-currency markets since 1972.

While final maturity is only a rough measure of credit exposure or the period during which the lender is committed to a given level of return on funds invested, Table F shows how radical variations in this key indicator can be over a limited period of time. While only a calculation

TABLE E   *Gross (Claims) and Net Exposure (Claims less Liabilities) of B.I.S.
Reporting Banks* to Selected Countries as of end-1978*
(in $ billions)

	Gross Exposure (Claims)		Net Exposure (Claims less Liabilities)
	Amount	*% of Total*	*Amount*
West Germany	50.2	5.6	22.2
Japan	39.0	4.3	27.1
Brazil	31.9	3.5	21.0
Italy	29.1	3.2	5.6
Mexico	23.4	2.6	17.0
Venezuela	13.1	1.5	3.6
Soviet Union	12.8	1.4	7.0
Denmark	11.9	1.3	7.3
Poland	11.7	1.3	10.9
Sweden	9.8	1.1	6.2
Norway	8.5	.9	5.1
South Africa	7.4	.8	6.4
South Korea	7.0	.8	4.5
Hungary	6.5	.7	5.5
German Democratic Republic	6.2	.7	5.0
Algeria	5.7	.6	3.0
Yugoslavia	5.6	.6	2.8
Finland	5.1	.6	3.5
Peru	3.4	.4	2.5
Turkey	3.0	.3	2.2
Grand Total	903.0		

Source: Bank for International Settlements

* The European reporting area (Belgium, Luxembourg, France, Germany, Italy,
Holland, Sweden, Switzerland, UK, Austria, Denmark and Ireland), Canada, US,
Japan, plus offshore US branches in the Bahamas, Cayman Islands, Panama, Hong
Kong and Singapore

of actual average life would give an accurate representation of the
maturity variable, the World Bank data shown in this table provides a
sufficiently valid approximation for comparison over a period of time.

Table F shows how sharp and cyclical variations in this indicator can
be over a period of years. Five sovereign borrowers which were
reasonably consistent takers of Euro-currency loans over the 1973–8
period have been selected for this purpose: the Banque Nationale
d'Algerie, Republic of Argentina, Government of Brazil, Imperial

TABLE F   *Final Maturity of Loans to Selected Major Euro-currency Borrowers January 1973– December 1979*

Borrower/Guarantor	Date of Offering		Final Maturity (years)
Republic of Argentina	1974	Feb	10
		June	8
		Oct	7
	1976	Nov	4
	1977	May	3
		June	5
		Oct	7
	1978	Jan	7
		Jan	5
		Feb	8
		Feb	5
		May	7
		June	4
		Aug	$8\frac{1}{2}$
		Sep	5
		Oct	8
		Nov	10
		Dec	10
		Dec	12
Bank Handlowy W. Warszawie SA (Poland) (direct and as guarantor)	1973	Apr	7
		May	10
		Oct	10
		Nov	7
		Dec	6
	1974	Feb	8
		Mar	8
		Apr	7
		July	7
		Sep	7
	1975	May	7
		June	5
		June	8
		Aug	7
	1976	Jan	5
		Feb	6
		May	7
		June	5
		Dec	7
	1977	Apr	5
	1978	Jan	8
		Mar	2
Banque Nationale d'Algerie	1973	Feb	10
		Aug	10

TABLE F   *(continued)*

Borrower/Guarantor		Date of Offering	Final Maturity (years)
Banque Nationale d'Algerie		Aug	15
	1975	Oct	7
	1976	May	5
		Nov	5
	1977	Sept	5
		Oct	5
	1978	June	6
		June	7
		June	6
		July	7
		July	7
		Oct	7
		Dec	7
Government of Brazil (direct or as guarantor)	1973	Mar	10
		Apr	10
		Sept	10
		Nov	15
	1974	Feb	12
		June	12
		Oct	10
		Dec	8
	1975	Jan	5
		Apr	5
		May	5
		June	5
		July	5
		Aug	5
		Aug	7
		Sept	5
		Oct	5
		Nov	5
		Dec	5
	1976	Jan	5
		Mar	5
		Apr	5
		Dec	7
		Dec	5
		Dec	6
		Dec	7
	1977	Jan	5
		June	5
		June	6
		June	6
		July	7

TABLE F   *(continued)*

Borrower/Guarantor		Date of Offering	Final Maturity (years)
Government of Brazil		Sept	5
(direct or as guarantor)		Sept	6
		Sept	7
		Sept	5
		Sept	7
		Dec	5
		Dec	7
		Dec	5
		Dec	5
		Dec	8
		Dec	5
	1978	Jan	8
		Jan	8
		Feb	8
		Mar	5
		Mar	7
		Apr	10
		Apr	5
		May	10
		June	10
		July	12
		July	10
		Aug	8
		Sept	10
		Sept	10
		Sept	12
		Sept	12
		Sept	10
		Oct	10
		Oct	12
		Oct	13
		Nov	10
		Nov	12
		Nov	15
		Nov	10
		Nov	12
		Dec	10
		Dec	12
		Dec	15
		Dec	10
	1973	Feb	8
Imperial Government of Iran		Mar	8
		Aug	10
		Oct	10

TABLE F   *(continued)*

Borrower/Guarantor	Date of Offering		Final Maturity (years)
Imperial Government of Iran	1976	June	7
		Dec	7
	1977	Dec	8
		Dec	7
	1978	June	10
		Sept	10

Source: *Borrowing in International Capital Markets*, World Bank Documents, EC—181.

Government of Iran and Bank Handlowy. Final maturities for the Government of Brazil, for example, rose to a high of fifteen years at the end of 1973, dropped to five years in 1975–6, and have since returned to the fifteen-year level at end 1978. While not as violent, swings in final maturity for the other borrowers were quite substantial reflecting competitive conditions and overall country debt service requirements rather than the cash flows from individual projects. Such fluctuations bring out the key importance of timing in building an international loan portfolio in that the relatively longer maturities generally incorporate a lower spread into which the lender is locked for the life of the loan.

Very few Euro-banks have established a permanent or semi-permanent maturity target, as expressed either in average life or ultimate maturity, which is built into the long term strategy of the bank. The great majority recognise their dependence on market conditions and inability to influence terms which in large part are established by larger banks in the market or 'competitive conditions'. Some chief executives go so far as to assume a passive role and to view their function as building a loan portfolio which reflects market conditions over an extended period of time. Others establish periodic guidelines which reflect both market conditions and the need to generate a certain minimum return on invested funds. During periods of vigorous competition for business such as existed in 1973/74 and again in 1978/79, such a guideline may have implied a virtual absence from the market, whereas in early 1975, with a more favourable risk/reward pattern for the lender, this type of guideline may have enabled the lender to shorten his average life considerably with a significant degree of selectivity.

A number of banks have established maximum permissible final maturities and average lives at levels of, respectively, ten years and five years or higher, but during less competitive periods such as early 1975 they were able to set provisional maxima well within these limits. Throughout the first half of 1975, for example, Euro-banks expressed almost unanimous agreement that an ultimate maturity of five years or possibly seven for selected project credits was the maximum acceptable, although many recognised that they might have to follow the market upward if the degree of competition increased. In the more competitive environment of 1979 with 10-year maturities again the norm, most Euro-banks admitted to a high degree of flexibility in interpreting their maturity guidelines. While reflecting the trend towards longer maturities and adopting a more restrictive lending posture as a result, few bankers are prepared to let maturity alone prevent them from making an otherwise attractive loan. A few banks have established fairly permanent guidelines within the overall maturity pattern; several insist on keeping a proportion—say one-third or one-half—of customer loans under one year in final maturity to provide an appropriate maturity balance and insure a certain loan run-off should spreads increase.

The actual level of average life in the summer of 1975 for Euro-banks appeared to range between two and four years with a heavy concentration around three years. Four years later it is likely that somewhat longer average portfolio lives were prevalent, although prepayments and a deliberate focus on short term paper offset this trend for many banks. In addition to the nature of the particular bank's asset portfolio, the timing of adding new loans on the books as indicated above is a highly relevant factor in determining this average.

The profitability of an individual loan or the portfolio as a whole is the final critical variable generally used to manage a Euro-bank loan portfolio. As in the case of maturity variability, loan spreads for comparable borrowers have fluctuated significantly during the past few years in response to a variety of factors which include credit as well as competitive considerations. Another component of loan profitability is represented by front end fees, which are particularly significant during lenders' markets and for credits which are relatively difficult to sell. Table G shows how, for the same borrowers as in the previous maturity analysis, interest margins over LIBOR (London Interbank Offered Rate) have moved for publicised credits since 1972 for the initial years of the outstanding loan. As in the case of Table F, a totally accurate calculation should include the amortisation over the life of the loan of various fees paid to the lenders, but as these fees tend to vary in line with the interest margin, the latter over time does provide an adequate comparative tool.

TABLE G *Initial Years' Interest Spread (over LIBOR) For Selected Major Euro-currency Borrowers, January 1973—December 1978*

Borrower/Guarantor	Date of Offering		Spread for initial years (%)
Republic of Argentina	1974	Feb	$1\frac{1}{2}$
		June	$1\frac{1}{2}$
		Oct	$1\frac{1}{2}$
	1976	Nov	$1\frac{7}{8}$
	1977	May	$1\frac{5}{8}$
		June	$1\frac{3}{4}$
		Oct	$1\frac{5}{8}$
	1978	Jan	$1\frac{1}{2}$
		Jan	$1\frac{1}{2}$
		Feb	$1\frac{3}{8}$
		Feb	$1\frac{1}{2}$
		May	$1\frac{1}{2}$
		June	$1\frac{1}{2}$
		Aug	$1\frac{3}{8}$
		Sept	$1\frac{1}{2}$
		Oct	$1\frac{3}{8}$
		Nov	$\frac{7}{8}$
		Dec	$\frac{7}{8}$
		Dec	$\frac{3}{4}$
Bank Handlowy W. Warszawie SA	1973	Apr	$\frac{5}{8}$
		May	$\frac{5}{8}$
(Poland) (direct and as guarantor)		Oct	$\frac{1}{2}$
		Nov	$\frac{5}{8}$
		Dec	$\frac{1}{2}$
	1974	Feb	$\frac{1}{2}$
		Mar	$\frac{7}{8}$
		Apr	$\frac{5}{8}$
		July	$\frac{5}{8}$
		Sept	1
	1975	May	$1\frac{1}{2}$
		June	$1\frac{1}{2}$
		June	$1\frac{3}{8}$
		Aug	$1\frac{1}{2}$
	1976	Jan	$1\frac{1}{2}$
		Feb	$1\frac{1}{2}$
		June	$1\frac{1}{2}$
		Dec	$1\frac{1}{2}$
	1977	Apr	$1\frac{1}{2}$

TABLE G (*continued*)

Borrower/Gurantor	Date of Offering		Spread for Initial Years (%)
	1978	Jan	$1\frac{3}{8}-1\frac{1}{2}$
		Mar	$1\frac{1}{4}$
Banque Nationale d'Algerie	1973	Feb	1
		Aug	$\frac{7}{8}$
		Aug	$1\frac{1}{8}$
	1975	Oct	$1\frac{1}{2}$
	1976	May	$1\frac{5}{8}$
		Nov	$1\frac{1}{2}$
	1977	Sept	$1\frac{5}{8}$
		Oct	$1\frac{5}{8}$
	1978	June	$1\frac{1}{2}$
		June	$1\frac{3}{8}$
		June	$1\frac{5}{8}$
		July	$1\frac{3}{8}$
		July	$1\frac{1}{4}$
		Oct	$1\frac{1}{4}$
		Dec	$1\frac{1}{4}$
Government of Brazil	1973	Mar	1
(direct or as guarantor)		Apr	1
		Sept	1
		Nov	$\frac{5}{8}$
	1974	Feb	$\frac{5}{8}$
		June	$\frac{3}{4}$
		Oct	$\frac{7}{8}$
		Dec	$1\frac{1}{2}$
	1975	Jan	$1\frac{3}{4}$
		Apr	$1\frac{3}{4}$
		May	$1\frac{3}{4}$
		June	$1\frac{3}{4}$
		July	$1\frac{3}{4}$
		Aug	$1\frac{3}{4}$
		Aug	$1\frac{1}{2}$
		Sept	$1\frac{3}{4}$
		Oct	$1\frac{3}{4}$
		Nov	$1\frac{3}{4}$
		Dec	$1\frac{3}{4}$
	1976	Jan	$1\frac{7}{8}$
		Mar	$1\frac{3}{4}$
		Apr	$1\frac{7}{8}$
		Dec	2

TABLE G (*continued*)

Borrower/Guarantor	Date of Offering		Spread for Initial Years (%)
Government of Brazil		Dec	$1\frac{7}{8}$
(direct or as guarantor)		Dec	$1\frac{7}{8}$
		Dec	$1\frac{15}{16}$
		Dec	$2\frac{1}{8}$
	1977	Jan	$1\frac{7}{8}$
		June	$1\frac{7}{8}$
		June	$1\frac{15}{16}$
		June	$1\frac{15}{16}$
		Sept	$1\frac{7}{8}$
		Sept	2
		Sept	$2\frac{1}{8}$
		Sept	$1\frac{7}{8}$
		Sept	$2\frac{1}{8}$
		Dec	$1\frac{7}{8}$
		Dec	$1\frac{7}{8}$
		Dec	$2\frac{1}{8}$
		Dec	$1\frac{7}{8}$
	1978	Jan	$2\frac{1}{8}$
		Jan	$2\frac{1}{8}$
		Feb	$2\frac{1}{8}$
		Mar	$1\frac{7}{8}$
		Mar	$2\frac{1}{8}$
		Apr	$1\frac{7}{8}$
		Apr	$1\frac{7}{8}$
		May	2
		June	$1\frac{1}{2}$
		June	2
		July	$1\frac{7}{8}$
		Aug	$1\frac{7}{8}$
		Sept	$1\frac{1}{8}$
		Sept	$1\frac{3}{8}$
		Sept	$1\frac{5}{8}$
		Sept	$1\frac{1}{4}$
		Sept	$1\frac{3}{8}$
		Oct	$1\frac{1}{8}$
		Oct	$1\frac{1}{4}$
		Oct	$1\frac{3}{8}$
		Nov	$1\frac{1}{8}$
		Nov	$1\frac{1}{4}$
		Nov	$1\frac{1}{2}$

Table G (*continued*)

Borrower/Guarantor	Date of Offering		Spread for Initial Years (%)
Government of Brazil		Nov	$1\frac{1}{4}$
(direct or as guarantor)		Nov	$1\frac{3}{8}$
		Dec	$1\frac{1}{8}$
		Dec	$1\frac{1}{4}$
		Dec	$1\frac{1}{2}$
		Dec	1
Imperial Government of Iran	1973	Feb	$\frac{3}{4}$
		Mar	$\frac{3}{4}$
		Aug	$\frac{5}{8}$
		Oct	$\frac{5}{8}$
	1976	June	$1\frac{3}{8}$
		Dec	$1\frac{1}{4}$
	1977	Dec	$\frac{7}{8}$
		Dec	$\frac{7}{8}-1$
	1978	June	$\frac{5}{8}-\frac{3}{4}$
		Sept	$\frac{5}{8}-\frac{3}{4}$

Source: *Borrowing in International Capital Markets,* World Bank Documents, EC—181.

During this six year period, interest margins for the Government of Brazil dropped to a low of $\frac{5}{8}$ per cent (for a 15-year maturity) in late 1973, rose sharply to a range of $1\frac{3}{4}-2\frac{1}{8}$ per cent (generally for 5–7-year maturities) for the 1975–7 period and then plummeted to the 1 per cent level at end-1978 (for a 10-year maturity), which represented the identical terms at which the five-year cycle had begun. A similar pattern was shown by the Imperial Government of Iran, whose spreads fell to $\frac{5}{8}$ per cent in late 1973, rose to $1\frac{3}{8}$ per cent in 1976 when the borrower once again came to the market, and fell steadily to a level of $\frac{5}{8}$ per cent in late 1978 just prior to the overthrow of the Shah when the borrower's name became unacceptable in the market. As pointed out previously, these variations reflect competitive conditions far more than perceptions of credit risk. What the above data do not show is the practice in 1978–9 of prepayment of the higher spread loans issued in the 1975–7 period which substantially diminished the benefits derived by those banks who deliberately built up their asset base in this period of cyclically high margins.

One of the unresolved issues in international lending is thus posed by the fact that, while pricing loans at a fixed margin over the cost of funds provides a theoretically assured gross margin, the practice of fixing a loan spread for a period of time which may exceed ten years substantially reduces the benefit of this innovation in loan pricing by preventing in most cases adjustments for changes in such critical variables as individual credit risk, rising operating costs or market conditions.

Within the constraints thus posed by the Euro-currency pricing formula and competitive conditions, many Euro-banks have responded by establishing fairly permanent minimum lending spreads (including front end fees amortised over the life of the loan) for medium-term loans so as to provide a minimum return on invested funds given certain assumptions of maximum gearing, operating costs, etc. The figure most often mentioned in this context is 1 per cent over LIBOR. A more flexible view is taken on short-term credits of up to one year, which can be regarded as providing incremental earnings until full gearing is achieved. In addition, special exceptions may be made for clients particularly close to the bank or its parents, and allowance is usually made for other income which may be derived from the same customer to offset an otherwise unacceptable loan spread. On top of this permanent minimum spread, such banks establish more temporary higher guidelines in the context of individual planning periods and current market conditions; in mid-1975, for example, a margin of $1\frac{1}{4}$ per cent—$1\frac{1}{2}$ per cent was regarded as the minimum acceptable for a prime credit on a medium-term basis. Some banks, on the other hand, feel that setting a target loan spread invites the taking of marginal credit risks, and a few of these banks refuse to consider loans with a spread exceeding a certain level on the assumption that a borrower paying more than a given interest margin is presumably not creditworthy.

A large number of Euro-banks, however, believe that establishing permanent guidelines which may force the bank out of the market for a period of time is not appropriate. In the view that they are a product of the market place, they believe that their performance can only be evaluated relatively in the context of that of similar banks rather than against an absolute standard of performance. Also, some managements feel that over an extended period of time the cycle of high and low spreads will average out to provide a reasonable return on invested funds without individual banks having to guess the timing of these moves. While such banks are prepared to establish provisional guidelines reflecting current market conditions, they take a much more flexible approach to the question of long-term loan profitability and often view the establishing of minimum acceptable spreads as wishful thinking.

In the highly competitive market of 1978/79, with loan spreads typically well below the minimum generally agreed necessary to provide an adequate return on funds employed, a flexible attitude to pricing was characteristic of the bankers interviewed. While substantially reducing their new commitments at these spread levels, Euro-banks are reluctant to set arbitrary minima which would preclude a transaction which in other respects was quite attractive.

The concept and adequacy of loan loss reserves is intimately related to management's policy with regard to loan profitability. While few Euro-banks are prepared to acknowledge that they are assuming anything but a first class credit risk in making a loan, the nature of much of the country and project lending of the late1970s, in addition to the actual or likely losses apparent on certain real estate and shipping loans made in the early to mid-1970s, have obliged many banks to look more closely at the adequacy of their available reserves to support a significant loss.

When asked in mid-1975 if they had in mind from a long-term, management planning standpoint a target loan loss reserve expressed presumably as a percentage of outstanding risk assets, somewhat over half of the Euro-bank executives felt that the concept was not relevant to their bank. These banks all acknowledged the necessity of reserving for specific realised or likely losses but felt that reserving additional, presumably taxed, amounts for management planning purposes was not valid. Many executives pointed out that all earnings would be retained in the bank for the foreseeable future to meet potential losses, and that, if these reserves were inadequate, the stockholders were capable of doing the necessary to restore the bank's viability. Several pointed to the excellent historical loss record in international lending and the difficulty of evaluating the ultimate loss potential inherent in possible country loan defaults.

The minority, who felt that a general loss reserve above and beyond specific experience was a valid concept, suggested percentage reserves that varied widely from $\frac{3}{4}$ per cent, which reflected domestic US experience, to 5 per cent, which presumed significant country loan losses. Most suggestions fell somewhat above or below $1\frac{1}{2}$ per cent of outstanding customer loans. Many of these banks voiced a general concern that newer banks without substantial retained earnings might well find it difficult to accumulate a sufficient cushion of such earnings in the event of an unexpected disaster early in their corporate lives.

When interviewed in mid-1979, the typical Euro-banker was still prepared to reserve only for specific likely or realised losses. On the other hand, an increasing number had begun to set aside taxed or untaxed general provisions from earnings as a result of pressure from stockholders, auditors or regulatory authorities as well as the recognition that the excellent historical record of international loan losses might not continue. Bankers who espoused this latter approach mentioned a wide range of desirable reserves but the one most frequently cited in mid-1979 was one of 1 per cent of risk assets.

In their efforts to develop their loan portfolios, Euro-banks rely to a widely varying extent on business provided by stockholders, loans generated by the Euro-bank's own management team, and business introduced from the market in the form of loan syndications. In many cases, it was pointed out that the distinction between the first two is tenuous at best in view of the close working relationship with the stockholders in dealing with joint customers. Slightly over half of the forty banks in the sample felt that business generated by their own efforts plus those of the stockholders accounted for at least one-half of the loans currently in their portfolios, whereas a few banks were totally or almost completely reliant on business brought them from other banks. Some Euro-banks have extensive new business development efforts based on overseas representative offices and calling programmes from London-based officers with geographic or functional responsibilities. Contributions of new business from parent banks of both wholly-owned and consortium Euro-banks varied from almost nothing to the bulk of the existing portfolio. The proportion of own-generated business seems to be more a function of the capabilities and preferences of the individual managements than any other factor.

In taking business from the market, most banks indicated that reciprocity was a significant factor assuming the credit and terms were reasonably acceptable; in a few cases the Euro-banks acknowledged that reciprocity was the principal reason for taking business from the market. Reciprocity in this context was measured by such factors as mutual interbank dealing relationships and willingness of the other bank to take loan syndications from the first bank.

In approving loan proposals, a variety of decision making procedures are utilised. At one extreme are the autonomous wholly-owned and consortium banks whose managements make all individual credit decisions without prior reference to non-executive members of the board of directors. At the other extreme are complex procedures of up to three or four ascending stages involving middle management, the chief executive, an executive committee of the board and the full board itself. In the case of wholly-owned subsidiaries, if reference to home office is necessary, a simple one-on-one contact between the chief executive and his organisational superior is usually sufficient. With consortium-owned banks, one or more stockholder representatives on the board are brought into the decision making process by the chief executive depending on the significance of the decision. For this purpose, the initial contact is often made by the chief executive with a committee based in London representing one or more of the stockholders which makes decisions on a quorum basis; for more significant decisions, a wider range of stockholder representatives may be contacted by telephone or telex; if one stockholder plays a dominant role in the consortium, a committee approach is often discarded.

The principal criterion determining reference to a higher authority than the chief executive is size of commitment. Many banks, however, also differentiate loan referrals on the basis of loan maturity, relationship to country limit and the presence of collateral security. Under these guidelines a chief executive will have greater autonomy, for example, if a given loan has a maturity of less than one year or if it is well within his country limit. Several chief executives emphasised the informal nature of the referral process to board members; particularly when a country risk or a customer known to a stockholder was involved, the chief executive preferred to share the decision with his executive committee even if the amount were well within his delegated limits.

The threshold amount beyond which the chief executives must refer a credit varies widely. In some cases the normal lending limit – say, 10–20 per cent of capital funds – can be committed by the chief executive, whereas in many consortium banks virtually all commitments of $1 million or more must be referred to a committee of the board.

In view of the number of changes in management and ownership as well as the wide variances in financial performance which took place in the 1975–79 period, emphasis was placed in the 1979 interviews on what changes, if any, had occurred in the decision-making structures of the bank as related to the credit process. In almost all cases, the actual structures in terms of involvement of various levels of management and Board had remained unchanged, while for most banks the actual limits delegated to the Chief Executive had increased in line with the growth of the bank and its capital funds. In many cases the arrival of a new chief executive was the occasion of a significant increase in these credit authorities. A major restructuring of stockholder interests has resulted in both increased and reduced delegated limits depending upon the policy of the new stockholders and their confidence in the management team. Typically, a new chief executive taking over after a period of significant loan losses has been able to secure an extension of his delegated authority. While in the smaller and medium sized Euro-banks there is relatively little lending authority delegated by the chief executive, in the larger ones with a growing network of officers around the world one finds increased delegation of authority to these units.

A final lending policy issue is the relative importance of fixed rate as opposed to floating-rate lending. For analytical purposes, I have defined fixed-rate lending as any asset, either loan or quoted security, which has a maturity significantly in excess of a deposit of matching maturity and is not held for trading purposes. When there is a customer demand for fixed-rate loans of up to five years and more and deposits can be obtained for equivalent maturities, Euro-banks have often engaged in this type of lending. On other occasions, Euro-banks have been prepared to take a view on rates by extending a medium-term loan at a fixed rate without taking a matching deposit; in addition, some Euro-banks have acquired fairly significant sterling long-date gilt edge portfolios for investment as opposed to trading purposes. In several cases such action was justified on the assumption that a portion of the bank's capital was being invested in quality, high yielding long-term assets. In practice, many of these quoted investments and offerings of fixed-rate loans were made in 1972–3 prior to the sharp world-wide upturn in interest rates in 1974, and enthusiasm for fixed-rate lending on an unmatched basis had diminished by mid-1975 to the extent that very few of the banks interviewed indicated any interest in becoming involved in the future. Bankers were quite reluctant to quantify the proportion of fixed-rate assets carried on their books, but in general it would appear that the amount of such loans for the typical Euro-bank is quite small.

4 Liability Management and Capital Adequacy

In addition to such traditional banking liability management challenges in the form of the appropriate mix of interest-bearing deposits to stockholders funds and the correct balance of money market involvement, the Euro-bank faces the additional issue of substantial dependence for its liabilities on an interbank market which, as the events of 1974 demonstrated, can be a highly volatile and uncertain source of funds. While the Euromarket loan pricing concept has simplified the banker's task of ensuring a relatively fixed gross interest margin on the bulk of his loan portfolio, a concept which does not exist in many national money markets, he cannot avoid the fact that he is essentially funding loans with an average life of perhaps three years with money market deposits of primarily three to six months in maturity.

Bank for International Settlements data perhaps best reflect the Euro-bank's almost complete dependence on interbank deposits as a source of funds. As of end-1978, only 12 per cent of reporting BIS countries' gross foreign currency liabilities were to non-bank institutions, down from 18 per cent in 1970.[1] The Euro-currency sector is acknowledged to be largely an interbank market, but the proportion of non-bank deposits available to Euro-banks is significantly less than that provided to the large US and continental banks in their home offices and London branches. Some indication of this is found in the Bank of England statistics which are summarised in Table H.

In early 1979, whereas the entire UK banking sector looked to the London interbank market for 21 per cent of its total sterling and foreign currency liabilities, consortium banks relied on the market for a total of 41 per cent of liabilities. In contrast, the London clearing banks were major net suppliers to the market, while their 17 per cent reliance on the interbank market by the American banks was somewhat below the sectoral average. In the case of most Euro-banks, a significant portion of 'other source' liabilities represents deposits from banks outside the UK banking sector; unfortunately, no published breakdown of overseas deposits by type of depositor is available.

TABLE H   *Composition of UK Banking Sector Liabilities as of 17 January 1979*
(amounts in £1000m.)

	Total Liabilities[a]		Of which				
			Sterling		Foreign Currency		
			From U.K. banking sector	Other sources	From U.K. banking sector		Other sources	
	Amount	% of Sector	Amount / % of Total sector	Amount / % of Total sector	Amount / % of Total sector	Amount / % of Total sector
Total Banking Sector	204.4	100.0	13.8 6.8	50.6[b] 24.8	28.1 13.7	112.0[b] 54.8
of which:						
London Clearing Banks	37.4	18.3	2.0 5.3	29.1 77.8	1.3 3.5	5.0 13.4
Accepting Houses	7.8	3.8	.9 11.5	2.8 35.9	1.2 15.4	3.0 38.5
American Banks	52.7	25.8	2.6 4.9	3.8 7.2	6.1 11.6	40.1 76.1
Japanese Banks	20.1	9.8	.3 1.5	.1 .5	4.3 21.4	15.3 76.1
Other Overseas Banks	44.1	21.6	2.1 4.8	2.8 6.3	7.4 16.8	31.8 72.1
Consortium Banks	8.9	4.3	.3 3.4	.3 3.4	3.3 37.1	5.0 56.2

Source: *Bank of England Quarterly Bulletin*, vol. 19, no. 1 (March 1979).

(a) Excluding items in suspense and transmission and capital and other funds.
(b) Includes Certificates of Deposit, some of which are held by other banks.

Behind this relatively low proportion of Euro-bank non-bank deposits lie such factors as the risk preference of major institutional and corporate depositors, the relative newness of most Euro-banks and the limited banking facilities they can offer to a corporate customer. The large multinational client has traditionally banked abroad with the overseas branches of his lead bank at home and/or a major local – i.e. UK – bank for a variety of subjective and objective reasons. Such a corporation places a high premium on the safety of its surplus funds and has usually proven reluctant to place funds with a lesser known bank despite a marginal yield advantage. Even other financial institutions such as central banks, insurance companies, and pension funds tend to place funds with the largest and best established London banks rather than go through the administrative procedure of verifying the credit standing of a relatively new and smaller Euro-bank. Normal commercial banking services such as money transfer, letters of credit, collections, and checking and payroll accounts for employees are much more efficiently handled by the large staffs of the London branches of UK banks than by a Euro-bank with a bare bones operational staff. Finally, the personal contacts which often lie behind the choice of a new bank take time to develop, and most Euro-banks are too new in the market to have established many such relationships.

One of the products of dependence on interbank funds is an aggravation of the maturity mismatch which has naturally arisen as loan maturities have been extended to periods of ten years and more. A most useful indicator of the extent of final maturity mismatching is provided by Bank of England data which analyse the net position by final maturity of assets and liabilities for periods ranging from call to over three years. Table I provides a comparison of this maturity analysis for the UK foreign currency banking sector as a whole and for the category of consortium banks, which represent a major component of the Euro-banking community, for selected dates during 1978. The data are shown as the net borrowed (−) or lent (+) position for the period expressed as a percentage of total liabilities to provide a proportional view of maturity mismatch. Maturities given are final, rather than roll-over period, maturities.

While both the industry and Euro-banks are net borrowers in the period from call to six months and generally lenders beyond this point, the net lending mismatch for Euro-banks is significantly larger than for the sector as a whole. In November 1978, for example, 22 per cent of the consortium banks' liabilities were represented by the excess of claims beyond three years over liabilities for the same period as opposed to only

TABLE 1   *Maturity Analysis of Net Foreign Assets and Liabilities of UK Banks: Net Position for Period as % of Total Liabilities*

Date	Call to 8 days Excl. C/Ds	Inc. C/Ds	Maturity Period 8 days to 1 Month	1 Month to 3 Months	3 Months to 6 Months	6 Months to 1 year	1 year to 3 years	Over 3 years
(1) Overall UK Banking Sector								
15 Feb 1978	(5.6)	(4.1)	(3.4)	(4.5)	(2.8)	(.2)	4.9	11.8
17 May 1978	(6.4)	(4.9)	(3.4)	(4.6)	(2.5)	(.6)	5.3	12.3
16 Aug 1978	(5.9)	(4.5)	(3.8)	(4.1)	(3.5)	(.3)	5.4	12.5
15 Nov 1978	(4.9)	(3.6)	(3.6)	(5.7)	(3.1)	(.1)	4.8	12.7
(2) Consortium Banks								
15 Feb 1978	(5.7)	(4.2)	(6.8)	(13.7)	(11.5)	1.6	17.0	21.5
17 May 1978	(4.9)	(3.2)	(8.3)	(15.3)	(11.5)	1.1	18.9	23.2
16 Aug 1978	(5.3)	(4.1)	(5.3)	(12.0)	(14.7)	1.6	17.3	21.1
15 Nov 1978	(6.1)	(4.7)	(7.4)	(13.2)	(12.0)	1.1	17.6	22.4

Source: *Bank of England Quarterly Bulletin*, vol. 19, no. 1 (March 1979).

13 per cent for the banking sector. These longer term claims, of course, generally represent the commitment period of a long-term loan priced on a roll-over basis. The relatively heavy mismatch for UK consortium banks in a sector already borrowing short and lending long probably reflects a combination of higher average life of loans and a relative lack of access to deposits of over three to six months.

The supply of interbank deposits thus available to Euro-banks fluctuates in size and character with the lending banks' posture towards interbank assets, current level of risk preference and their source of funds. While the typical interbank deposit has a maturity of three, six or twelve months which corresponds to the standard roll-over periods for Euro-currency loans, much longer deposits are available periodically in the market with maturities of up to five years or more. These latter tend to be placed with large US, UK and European banks, and in moments of market nervousness are rarely offered to Euro-banks. The London branches of large American banks and other UK and Continental banks which are the largest net lenders to the Euro-banks are often influenced in their placing of deposits by home office policy. At the end of 1974, for example, when US banks were under pressure to reduce balance sheet growth, interbank assets placed in the Euro-currency market in many cases were substantially reduced. During periods of market nervousness when there is significant pressure to take action against possible losses on interbank loans, extension of credit to smaller and newer banks tends to be the first to be cut back.

On the other hand, until mid-1974 these banks, in the context of building larger asset and earnings bases, were often prepared to lend on an interbank basis with relatively little financial analysis or personal knowlege of the borrowing bank and in amounts which bore little relationship to the latter's resources, on the implicit assumption that a participant in the market possessed sufficient capital resources, support from stockholders or a potential call on Central Bank assistance to be able to meet its obligations. A substantial portion of the interbank segment of the Euro-currency market's growth in the early 1970s was undoubtedly due to the ease with which relative newcomers to the market could tap the market for substantial amounts without provoking the questions which would have been asked of a corporate borrower. While many banks had always done a conscientious job of analysing their interbank commitments, the failure of the US National Bank of San Diego in 1973 followed by that of Franklin National Bank and Bankhaus I. D. Herstatt in mid-1974 provoked a widespread and sudden awareness – and often exaggeration – of the risks in lending to any but the very largest and best banks in the international system.

The significance of the latter two failures went well beyond the actual losses suffered. Franklin's demise shook bankers' confidence in the safety of physical size; Franklin's assets of $5,000 million made it one of the top twenty American banks. While Herstatt had long had a reputation for heavy exchange dealing in relation to its capital, the German bank's failure focused attention on the intra-day risk of spot exchange transactions, which had been regarded by many bankers as virtually riskless. Millions of dollars were lost by banks which had delivered Deutsche Marks to Herstatt in the morning to be covered by an expected delivery of the cover in dollars in New York a few hours later – delivery which was never made because of the bank's closure before the New York opening.

Following a wave in the second half of 1974 of rumours about the real and presumed difficulties of the smaller and newer members of the fraternity, which included a large number of the Euro-banks under discussion, what appeared to be a balance between reckless growth and sheer unreason was reached by mid-1975. A few Euro-banks were obliged to sell significant amounts of assets to parent banks because of inability to fund themselves, and a much larger number had recourse to informal stockholder support through direct funding, but no Euro-banks in my sample were reported to have been unable to meet their interbank obligations. The upsets of 1974 have brought in their train greater personal contact between lenders and borrowers in the interbank market, a more structured decision making process with regard to the granting of interbank lines and a greater awareness on all sides of the limitations of reliance on the interbank market. In the period to mid-1979, a relatively liquid interbank market prevailed as a result of such factors as Central Bank identification of parental responsibility for Euro-banks, the increased availability of funds, satisfactory performance by Euro-banks and the absence of bank collapses which resulted in depositor losses.

An understanding of the decision-making process in the granting of interbank lines is thus critical to an appreciation of the liability management strategy of the Euro-bank. Technically, interbank lines are undisclosed and uncommitted internal guidance lines establishing the maximum amount and maturity of funds a bank may be prepared to lend another bank. Though theoretically undisclosed, most Euro-banks become reasonably well aware of the existence and often amount of these lines through observance of the deposits appearing – or not appearing – on their books and the informal market chatter which takes place with other bank dealers. A typical Euro-bank may have lines for several hundred other banks, which in itself represents a significant administrative burden. These banks are selected on the basis of presumed creditworthiness, personal and corporate relationships, the other bank's activity in the market, reciprocity in dealing, and the presence of other business relationships. Having determined from an analysis of these considerations that a line should be granted, management usually fixes the size of the line on the basis of the taking bank's capital.

Most Euro-banks interviewed use 5–20 per cent of the borrower's net worth as a standard which could be adjusted up or down by special circumstances; a figure of 10 per cent was the one most often mentioned as a standard maximum. Smaller banks tend to establish a maximum absolute line they will grant of, say, up to $5 million, while many banks will not lend more than their capital to any other institution regardless of the latter's size and creditworthiness. Quite often borrowing banks will be split into two or more categories of creditworthiness; the top market category can be granted funds for up to twelve months or more, with three or six months being regarded as the maximum exposure for the lesser categories. Lines for spot and forward foreign exchange dealing may be granted almost automatically as a multiple of perhaps four times the deposit dealing lines, although some banks regard this as a completely separate management decision. A number of Euro-banks, in addition, establish a maximum daily delivery exposure combining both foreign exchange and deposit liabilities which will fix a maximum possible exposure to non-payment on any given day resulting from cumulative deposit and foreign exchange obligations outstanding on that day. In the case of many wholly-owned subsidiaries and a few consortium banks, the Euro-bank subsidiary is granted a portion of a global line established for the borrowing institutions by the parent or parents.

On the other hand, a relatively small number of Euro-banks still determine their interbank line exposure without fixed guidelines. To these banks more subjective factors such as personal relationships, usage by the other bank and reciprocity are the vital factors in establishing and modifying an interbank dealing relationship.

In particular since the formalisation of the interbank dealing decision-making process which began in mid-1974, the management of most Euro-banks has devoted a significant amount of time to the task of establishing, restoring and possibly increasing the lines it is granted from other banks. Liability management has thus often become synonymous with the maintenance of one's market reputation and borrowing base provided by other bankers. In the greater era of frankness engendered by the problems of 1974 and the universal acknowledgment of dependence on the interbank market, the Euro-bank manager discusses more freely with potential lending banks his asset strategy, the degree of parent support and in particular any significant problems he may have in his loan portfolio. Euro-banks also are less hesitant about invoking overall relationships, including that of their parent institutions, to bring about the desired result of obtaining or retaining an interbank line.

One of the consequences of the sharpened perception of vulnerability to the vagaries of the interbank market has been the focus on parent bank support of their Euro-bank offspring. At their inception, most Euro-banks were provided with publicised or informal lines of credit, often a multiple of their capital funds, from parent institutions. In the turmoil of 1974, the adequacy of even this level of support was called into question, and in the context of an international Central Bank programme of delineation of responsibility, the Bank of England in late 1974 requested and received letters of support from Euro-bank stockholders which implied a level of moral support going beyond their strictly legal commitments to a limited liability company. While most Euro-bankers considered such a letter an unnecessary restatement of the óbvious, this action by the Bank of England in all likelihood contributed to a restoration of market confidence.

Another consequence of the events of 1974 for liability management has been the phenomenon of tiering, or differentiation of rates paid by different banks for interbank deposits. Whereas little if any differentiation in the London Interbank Offered Rate (LIBOR) was made previously among banks, the heightened sensitivity to relative creditworthiness created a situation in 1974 whereby certain categories of banks were expected to pay a premium over the offered rate whose level was dependent upon their presumed creditworthiness. Hence, 'Japanese', 'Italians', 'consortia' and 'small merchants' found themselves asked to pay a premium for funds which not only directly reduced their gross interest spread but also implicitly impugned their credit standing. The almost universal reaction among Euro-banks, which were among those most affected by the tiering of rates, was not to pay 'over the odds' on the reasonable assumption that such a concession would either confirm the lender's view of relative creditworthiness or lead to a higher premium being asked on the subsequent occasion – or both! As in the case of one's lending record, one's ability to resist paying a premium for funds became a symbol of manhood in the Euro-market, and there well may be a difference between the reality of rates paid and the claims of a bank's management anxious to confirm the bank's reputation. To the extent that funds have been declined by management because of the premium requested, Euro-banks have been forced to restrict asset growth, run involuntary deposit mismatch positions or call on parental assistance. In the period of relative calm which characterised the interbank market in 1976–79, the extent of tiering declined substantially.

While the successive shocks administered in 1974 to the interbank market resulted in a salutory rationalisation of interbank lending practices and other positive benefits, it also pointed up the key role which confidence – and lack of it – plays in the Euromarket. The boom of 1972–3 with its sense of permanent upward momentum, large dealing positions and heavy volume almost overnight gave way to widespread gloom which envisaged not only the disappearance of many Euro-banks but also the possible drying up of the Euro-market or its replacement by a club of a few dozen of the largest banks who alone would be able to attract funds. In the event, a combination of good sense, action by the relevant authorities and the natural flow of funds from low to high yielding employment righted the ship in late 1974. While there is no assurance this confidence cycle will not be repeated, Euro-bank managements are now equipped with defensive techniques of liability management which should prove useful if the cycle should repeat itself.

The turmoil of 1974 also focused management attention on the desirability of greater reliance on customer deposits to diminish the absolute and relative dependence on the interbank market. With the exception of several Euro-banks who operate virtually as the London branch of their parents, these institutions as pointed out previously rarely have a significant natural customer deposit base. A fairly large minority of the Euro-banks interviewed expressed the view that building a customer deposit base was neither realistic nor particularly desirable in view of their inability to provide the facilities necessary to adequately service corporate or individual deposits, their parents' greater capabilities and presumed preference to handle this business themselves, and the greater inclination by these depositors since the events of 1974 for the safety of the very largest banks. Even if sizable customer deposits were obtained, these banks feel that their ultimate fate in a repetition of the 1974 crisis would still be in the hands of other banks as some degree of dependence on interbank funds will inevitably exist.

On the other hand, a majority of the banks interviewed placed a fairly high priority on building a customer deposit base despite the acknowledged difficulties for most banks in achieving any degree of success. Such banks pointed to the relative stability of these deposits, the ability in some cases to pay lower rates than in the interbank market because of close relationships or the relatively small size of individual deposits, and the cushion even a small portion of these deposits would provide in offsetting the fluctuations in sentiment and volume of the interbank market.

While no particularly useful published data are available, in practice the Euro-banks interviewed in mid-1975 held proportions of customer deposits which ranged from zero to over 60 per cent of total liabilities. The average bank characterised its customer proportion as 'very small', which appears in practice to approximate 10–20 per cent of the total. At the low end of the scale are some of the newest banks and those who make no effort to attract such deposits, while at the other extreme are the consortia and wholly-owned subsidiaries who function effectively as London branches of the parent organisation with a number of long standing customers of the parent who deposit regularly at the subsidiary bank, presumably with the active encouragement of the stockholder institutions. Banks with a regional character generally attract central bank and other funds, often in large amounts, from the particular region. Some of the larger and better established banks bid actively and successfully for deposits of large multinational corporations. When interviewed in mid-1979, the great majority of banks reported that non-interbank deposits continued to represent a nominal portion of the total, although a few reported significant progress in building a customer deposit base.

Banks with sectoral specialisation in energy and shipping also attract deposits from these sectors, with the latter able to command often substantial aggregate amounts through charter retention accounts in connection with secured loans outstanding. In most cases, deposits from customers of the parent banks provide a significant percentage of total non-interbank deposits, whereas the direct efforts of the Euro-bank itself to attract funds from depositors unconnected with the group have had limited success.

Another facet of liability management which received special attention during the 1974 crisis of confidence is the generally accepted principle that a Euro-bank must appear both as a lender and taker of interbank funds despite the general recognition of the low, if non-existent, profitability of interbank loans for these banks and their acknowledged net dependence on this source of funds. With a few exceptions in the form of banks who considered such a two-way activity to be purely cosmetic and unnecessary, all the banks interviewed expressed the view that an undefined and presumably flexible percentage of their borrowings should be relent in the interbank market. Apart from the understandable desire to provide balance sheet liquidity and balance and to maintain the professional objective of at least occasionally making two-way prices, those Euro-banks seemed to be responding to an often explicit criticism by the large net lenders that 'certain banks' were only takers and therefore not making a contribution to the market. The few banks who were prepared to quantify the relationship between interbank assets and interbank liabilities spoke in terms of 20–30 per cent of the latter being reinvested in the market. The view is often expressed that those banks which were active lenders as well as takers in the interbank market fared better during the 1974 funding crisis than those which simply funded their own loan portfolio.

As the preceding analysis indicates, funding a Euro-bank's loan portfolio and providing in addition funds for liquidity and/or interbank lending is almost invariably the principal mission of the bank's dealing room. In the case of a few wholly-owned subsidiaries, funding has actually been assigned to the local branch of the parent bank to minimise operating costs and obtain funds at the (presumably lower) parent's cost of money. In a somewhat larger number of cases, the chief executive has established funding as the sole objective of the dealing team with no expectation of profit from deposit dealing or foreign exchange operations or willingness to take the positions necessary to obtain such profits. Implicit in this position is the view that parent banks are better placed to take a view on deposit and exchange rates and that the Euro-bank's *raison d'etre* is making loans rather than speculating on interest and exchange rates.

In the great majority of the banks interviewed, however, the dealing room is expected to turn a gross profit before expenses in deposit dealing or foreign exchange trading or, in most cases, both. In a relatively small number of banks, in particular those with continental European patronage, maintaining dealing positions on which a profit was expected was regarded as a key element of the bank's strategy and a traditional aspect of international banking.

Recognising that profitability in a deposit or exchange dealing situation implies an interest rate or exchange rate risk, the majority of Euro-banks thus are prepared to take a view on the future of Euro-currency interest and/or exchange rates in what they consider are reasonable amounts over reasonable periods of time. To a certain extent, this view may be the involuntary consequence of factors beyond the Euro-bank's control.

In the interbank deposit market, a matching deposit for a given loan may not be available in the right amount or at the right rate for several days following a loan rate fixing, and during periods of market stress as in 1974, involuntary mismatching was much more extensive. Correspondingly, in the exchange market, a counterpart for an exchange order executed on behalf of a good customer may not be available immediately so that a temporary exchange position may develop.

To a significant extent, however, voluntary positions are taken on the basis of a management view of interest rates or exchange movements. If a downward trend in interest rates is foreseen, a bank may fund a six month maturity roll-over loan with a one or three month deposit to benefit from the prospect of renewing the latter at a lower cost. In the exchange market, an outright forward position may be taken in anticipation of an exchange rate movement, or a swap effected to benefit from an expected movement in relative interest rates of two Euro-currencies.

Of the Euro-banks which acknowledge a profit objective for their dealing rooms, a number feel very strongly that setting any explicit profit targets for dealing earnings (above and beyond the presumed loan spread over LIBOR and presumed earnings on invested capital) and exchange profits is mistaken in that it encourages dealers to take unnecessary risks to achieve the desired level of profits. Most dealers in the Euro-market, with some reason in the light of the losses which have taken place in recent years, are most reluctant to commit themselves in a planning context to anything more than a modest profit goal. Of the banks which were prepared to quantify their profit goals, a range of 1/8 per cent to 3/8 per cent minimum margin on the relevant deposit base seemed to be anticipated on the interbank lending book as representing the profit from running a successful mismatch position, as well as any earnings from matching deposits at a profit. As explained earlier, significant matched profits on deposits are rare in view of the need by most Euro-banks to pay approximately the offered rate at which their loans were priced.

In the light of the massive acknowledged foreign exchange losses by some of the world's largest banks in recent years since the abandonment of fixed parities and the totally unexpected interest rate movements in major currencies during periods such as mid-1974, earning a dealing profit in the mid-1970s represents a major achievement. While, for

example, one could conceive of at least a marginal profit being made on
a deposit mismatch over an extended period of time due to the normal
slant of a yield curve, a number of mechanistic or formula approaches
on an *ex-post* basis over the last decade would have produced overall
losses rather than the expected profit. It should be emphasised, however,
that mismatch policy remains for most Euro-banks a subjective,
unquantified decision-making process.

The difficulty of managing such positions is complicated by the fact
that few chief executives of Euro-banks have an extensive background in
the dealing function. Even if this were the case, instances of unauthorised dealing or even fraud in the case of non-Euro-banks in recent
years have confounded some of the best personal and procedural
monitoring systems.

As is generally recognised, a deposit mismatch position involves both
a liquidity and a profit risk. The former would exist in the case of a
'normal' mismatch whereby a given loan is funded by a shorter deposit
which must be rolled over before maturity of the asset. The profit risk in
such a case would be realised if interest rates were to rise, forcing the
bank to pay a higher rate when the shorter deposit was renewed. To the
extent that a deposit mismatch position is permitted, there is a fairly
distinct split in philosophy. On the one hand, some chief executives
control the position by close personal inspection of the daily liquidity
position and maturity ladder and frequent consultation with the dealers
without the use of formal numerical guidelines. These liquidity ladders
list by time period total net cash flow, usually daily for the forthcoming
week or fortnight followed by longer periods beyond this point. By
inspection a dealer can determine the amount of funds necessary to
cover a given negative position or put out in the market a projected
surplus.

On the other hand, roughly half of the banks which authorise
mismatch positions establish guidelines based on maximum quanti-
tative exposure and duration of exposure. The former control is derived
from the liquidity motive and relates to the theoretical need in an
emergency to raise funds to cover a net borrowed position in a limited
period of time. Several banks have in mind an amount, unrelated to
capital or deposits, which they could borrow from the market or
stockholders in an emergency; this amount places a theoretical ceiling
on the mismatch position. Some banks express this amount in terms of
available liquid resources, such as holdings of certificates of deposit or
rediscountable assets which must cover a net borrowed position over a
given period. Other banks set an absolute or relative amount, such as 10

per cent of deposits or a major fraction of their capital, which is to a certain extent an approximation of the funds they could obtain from the market in an emergency to cut out a borrowed position.

A relatively smaller number of banks limit the maximum period from the spot date that a mismatch can be run, such as three or six months, to protect primarily against the interest rate risk which is presumed to increase geometrically over time. Within this period, absolute or relative limits are often placed either on the cumulative mismatch – specifically net borrowed – position at any given date plus any period of a few weeks within that period which may have to be covered.

Foreign exchange activity may include relatively passive operations such as covering spot or forward exchange orders given by customers and generating a deposit for lending purposes in a given currency through a covered swap out of another currency. It also may involve spot-forward or forward-forward transactions for interest rate arbitrage purposes where the dealer anticipates a differential interest rate movement between the currencies. Finally, outright spot or forward positions may be taken when the dealer anticipates a differential movement in exchange rates. While usually pointing out that any such outright positions were relatively small and infrequent, roughly half of the banks running a dealing function are prepared to take such positions. In only a small number of cases did the bank establish modest profit targets for the foreign exchange function, although most banks expected this function to turn at least a small profit before expenses.

For the banks which were prepared to take a position risk, a minority of chief executives use no guidelines for controlling the position but instead rely on close personal contact with the dealers, regular examination of actual spot and forward positions and direct instructions to take or cut out a position. The majority, however, use a fairly standard control format which places limits by each dealing currency on the spot open position, spot against overall forward position and individual open positions within the forward ladder. The latter control is considered desirable as an overall forward position may be balanced but contain within the maturity ladder an otherwise hidden contract to sell a currency on one forward date and buy it back on another, thereby exposing the bank to an exchange risk at the first maturity. An overall spot or forward maximum position for all currencies combined is often applied. In addition, a weighting system placing a higher weight over time may be used to limit forward-forward exposure. In the case of some wholly-owned subsidiaries which form part of a world-wide network, the parent home office establishes these guidelines on the basis of usage, the affiliate's track record and the parent's view of relative dealing capabilities. In some cases intra-day limits are imposed, but most banks control their spot and forward exposure on a close of business basis. While very few absolute limits were cited, those mentioned represented a fairly small percentage of capital funds – say $1–2 million for spot open positions by currency.

A significant source of exchange dealing profits for several Euro-banks is the making of a market in a secondary currency which happens to be that of one of its parent banks. By utilising their parent bank's dealing position in that currency as a counterpart and backstop, these banks are often the principal London market makers in currencies such as Italian lire, Swedish kroner, Spanish pesetas and Mexican pesos.

While available published information does not permit any serious analysis of the record of Euro-banks in achieving deposit mismatch and foreign exchange profits, the absence of any major publicised problems in this sector for Euro-banks and the willingness of most banks to continue these operations seems to indicate that experience has been reasonably successful. Most Euro-bankers privately admit that mis-match results in 1974 were not particularly good due to the unexpected upward movement in dollar interest rates, but significant profits were generally made during the subsequent decline to mid-1975. Euro-bankers note with a certain satisfaction that the well publicised foreign exchange losses due to fraud and unauthorised dealing occurred in the largest and presumably most experienced banks in the market rather than among the Euro-banks. Only one of the forty banks interviewed admitted to a significant exchange dealing loss, which resulted in the termination of key staff.

Over the 1975–9 period, relatively few banks significantly modified their deposit and F/X dealing limits. Some increased these limits in view of the bank's growth, but others actually cut back as dealing activity was reduced.

The adequacy of a Euro-bank's capital and the appropriate level of gearing (leverage) has been an issue which aroused heated argument in the London market in the mid-1970s. Gearing is defined here as total deposits divided by total capital funds, including subordinated debt and non-specific reserves. While no official published data exist, the sample of forty banks whose results are analysed in Chapter 6 had an arithmetic average gearing as of their fiscal 1978 year end of 15.2 times capital funds. This average, however, included several banks in the 24–28 range and a number with leverage of only 5–8 times capital. Euro-banks with relatively high ratios often point to the support of their parent institutions and in many respects consider themselves an extension of the financial resources of their much larger parents; others justify their higher ratios on the basis of the quality of their asset portfolio. While the older and larger banks tend to have higher ratios which were built up during a boom market period when funds availability was taken for granted and leverage was regarded less critically, many of the newer and smaller banks have found their growth automatically constrained by the market's unwillingness to extend interbank lines despite receipt of parent support letters by the Bank of England.

The actual size of total capital funds for the sample ranges from £4.3 million to £96.6 million with an arithmetic average of about £19 million. Included in this capital base is frequently found subordinated debt provided by stockholders; in large part as a result of market and Bank of England pressure, much of this subordinated debt has been converted to equity. Some wholly-owned subsidiary Euro-banks have actually reduced their capital base since 1975 as a result of a change in strategy away from the lending function.

When questioned as to what they considered an appropriate maximum leverage for their own bank, most chief executives referred to the Bank of England guidelines discussed below. Some were frank to point out that, given the composition and quality of their asset base or the strength of their stockholders, they would strive to achieve as high a level of leverage as permitted by the Bank of England and the market itself. Of the majority of the bankers prepared to express a specific view in 1979, maximum ratios of 15–30:1 were mentioned. The most frequently mentioned ratio was 20:1, which represents a significant increase from the 15:1 generally cited in the 1975 interviews. Most of the relatively undergeared banks in 1975 had moved upwards toward the mean while several of the most highly geared institutions had somewhat reduced their leverage by 1979 as a result of factors which included pressure from the Bank of England.

The approach of the Bank of England to the issue of capital adequacy is based on an evaluation of the individual circumstances of each bank, its business and its management examined individually by Bank of England personnel over a period of time. In the mid-1970s, a continuous dialogue, intense at times, has taken place between the Bank and individual Euro-banks which were regarded as having unduly high leverage on the basis of the bank's analysis of these factors. As outlined by the Bank in September 1975:

it is recognised as inappropriate to attempt to quantify precise ratios between balance sheet aggregates; such quantification would lead to insufficient flexibility both between banks or categories of banks at any one time and for any particular bank in different circumstances. It should nevertheless be possible to develop over time broad numerical standards for the different groups of banks which may be used as yardsticks.[2]

While allowing for differences between categories of banks and among banks within the same category, the Bank of England has attempted to establish a relationship between deposit and acceptance liabilities on the one hand and free capital (defined as stockholders' funds less fixed assets and other elements of a bank's infrastructure) on the other. A sophisticated effort is being made to analyse the risk element in various types of assets. On the basis of this analysis, it is believed that the Bank regards a gearing range of 15–20:1 as appropriate for Euro-banks in general.

In Luxembourg, the banking authorities have taken the view that stockholder funds should represent a minimum of 3 per cent of liabilities, or a 33:1 gearing ratio. In contrast, the Hong Kong authorities have adopted a more liberal approach to such guidelines.

5 Fee-Earning and Other Activities

While a number of the earliest Euro-banks were established in the mid-1960s largely to participate in the medium-term lending function of the Euro-currency market, several factors have led to an increasing focus on investment or merchant banking and related activities. American and Japanese commercial banks saw in the establishment of overseas subsidiaries a means of engaging in investment banking activities prohibited in their domestic markets. Other banks already carrying on such activities followed their clients into the international capital markets through their Euro-bank affiliates. An all-pervasive influence, however, has been the increasing awareness of most Euro-banks that income derived independently of a capital base was one of the few means by which a Euro-bank beset by rapidly rising costs of operation, limited lending spreads and a presumed leverage ceiling could produce a reasonably attractive return on stockholder funds.

One of the first and most logical merchant banking activities has been the management or co-management of syndicated Euro-currency loans, an activity in which the Euro-bank can combine its balance sheet strength, financial packaging skills and marketing talents to earn management or front end fees. The size and frequency of these fees has been a function of market competitiveness and the attractions of the particular piece of business. During the borrower's markets of 1973 and 1978/79, a treasurer of a prime multinational corporation or a governor of a well-regarded Central Bank would become his own investment banker and bring together a willing group of lenders without anyone daring to suggest that a significant front end fee was appropriate. In contrast, during the lender's market of early 1975, management fees for less popular country credits rose to 1 per cent flat and more and were split among the originator, several co-managers who committed for a portion of the placement, and participants who simply signed on the dotted line. To varying degrees almost all Euro-banks have participated in the origination or placing of syndicated loans. Parent company customers and borrowers from the countries sponsoring particular Euro-banks represent the most logical candidates for loan origination. So-called market business, primarily foreign government or agency borrowers who come to the market frequently, represent a major target of opportunity for any Euro-banker prepared to travel to the borrower's capital, establish his credentials and make an underwriting or best efforts offer to place the borrower's next loan. To many government and official agency borrowers in the less-developed countries with more or less permanent borrowing requirements, the principal considerations in choosing offers have been the relative attractiveness of term, amount and ability of the Euro-bank to produce results rather than any consideration of past or future relationship. In 1978 alone, for example, there were 68 different publicised loans for Brazilian borrowers alone, of which 36 different loans were placed during the year for the central government or under its guarantee.[1]

Among the Euro-banks which have taken a leading role in syndication in the 1970s have been the Euro-bank subsidiaries of large American banks with world-wide networks to generate and monitor business and substantial balance sheets enabling them to carry a large portion of the loan. Specialised London-based subsidiaries of these banks are primarily engaged in packaging and selling Euro-currency loans; the bulk of their earnings is derived from fee income, as its share of the loan as a manager or co-manager is usually taken on the books of the larger parent organisation. Some major consortium Euro-banks have also been heavily engaged in managing loans, often committing firm for substantial amounts which could be taken by stockholder banks if unplaced outside the group. The placement process varies according to the size and complexity of the loan involved, but for a 'name' risk such as a well known government or agency hundreds of potential participating banks might be approached by telex and accept in principle by the same means. A Euro-bank's stockholders represent a natural source of placing power, although appetites of individual stockholder banks vary widely. A smaller or complex loan, however, might be discussed verbally with a limited number of potential participants prior to the sending of a telex or offering prospectus.

During the borrower's markets of 1973 and 1978/79 market conditions encouraged originating banks to commit firm for substantial amounts, often in excess of their capital, to secure a highly desired piece of business in the face of competition prepared to do the same. When the market broke in 1974, however, many large deals which carried pre-crisis pricing had to be held in portfolio with the result that funding problems were aggravated at a difficult moment and already narrow spreads were eroded by the tiering of LIBOR.

The willingness of Euro-banks to underwrite an amount in excess of their intended ultimate participation is quite mixed. Somewhat over half of the banks polled were prepared to underwrite an amount in excess of that which they intended to take as a participant in the credit. In most cases, a multiple of two or three times the latter was considered a reasonable underwriting maximum. Quite often a substantial loan amount will be underwritten formally or informally by one or more stockholder banks along with the Euro-bank itself; such a decision would usually be taken at board level and might well involve as the borrower a customer of one of the stockholder banks. In other cases, a bank will either take market soundings on a 'no-name' basis or actually pre-place on an 'approval subject to documentation' basis with a number of other friendly banks.

The financial and visual benefits of originating a successful Euro-currency loan are obvious; the originating bank generally retains a portion of the management fee or override for itself as well as appearing as lead or agent bank in the publicity tombstone. For a bank unable or unwilling to originate business, a co-manager or sub-underwriting role can also bring a useful share of the management fee as well as a possible special bracket position in the tombstone. Unlike the Euro-bond market, the unsold portion of the loan can be taken into portfolio without carrying the interest rate risk implicit in a fixed interest obligation.

With the intense competition for management positions from the major national banks in Japan, Europe and Canada prevalent in the 1978/79 borrowers' market, the profit potential for a Euro-bank without support from asset-hungry stockholders was substantially reduced. Relatively unattractive risk/reward relationships coupled with thin management fees meant relatively small sell-downs through pool syndication with the result that most Euro-banks found it very difficult in the period to maintain their level of fee income from syndication unless they were willing to absorb large portions of their underwriting commitments.

A second major investment banking activity of many Euro-banks is participation in the Euro-bond fixed rate publicly quoted securities and private placement markets. With an annual new issue volume which has ranged since 1968 from $3,000 million to $18,000 million,[2] the Euro-bond market has been more volatile and smaller in volume of new issues than the Euro-currency market but represents a major source of funds for certain international borrowers. These tend to be prime, well-known government and corporate names with a credit rating superior to many borrowers in the Euro-currency market. Underwriting and selling commissions are somewhat higher than is the case in the US.

The two key elements to a successful Euro-bond operation are acknowledged to be good placing power in the sector of primary (new) issues and the ability to reduce one's portfolio to minimise losses if a secondary trading portfolio is maintained. While the markets have grown and matured considerably in the late 1970s, there is relatively little institutional support compared with most large national bond markets, and ultimate holders tend to be largely individuals whose portfolios in many cases are managed for them by Swiss and other banks. Interest rate movements and investors' currency predilections tend to be major factors behind Euro-bond price movements as opposed to underlying security values, as many investors use Euro-bonds as a vehicle for taking a view on exchange and interest rates. The secondary market has been criticised for its thinness and inability to reflect these underlying security values.

The advent of floating currency rates has played a significant role in determining the character of the Euro-bond market as well as its attractiveness to Euro-banks. When exchange rate uncertainty was added to interest rate volatility, the Euro-bond market became less attractive as an investment market, and in the view of many observers both the primary and secondary markets, in which many Euro-banks participate, have suffered accordingly.

The Euro-banks interviewed split about equally between those who are active participants in at least one phase of the market and those who deliberately avoid any significant involvement. Those who participate range from banks who are active in all phases of origination, management, distribution and secondary market dealing to others who participate only as members of underwriting or selling groups or as secondary market traders. A number of Euro-banks, including both wholly-owned subsidiaries as well as consortia, point out that the Euro-bond market represented their first objective and initial activity in London with Euro-currency lending growing up subsequently. Those banks who have started from scratch in recent years in the Euro-bond market have begun generally by building a secondary trading capability or by developing primary placing power and using either or both of these strengths to work into underwriting and selling groups.

Between the 1975 and 1979 interviews, a number of Euro-banks—in particular subsidiaries of large US institutions—placed substantial additional resources behind their securities functions in a conscious effort to compete with the European universal banks and US investment banks. On the other hand, a few others during this period reduced or eliminated their Euro-bond activity because of poor profits performance.

Chief executives whose banks are active in the market emphasise the need to participate in capital as well as lending market activities to be able to offer a full range of investment and commercial banking services to their clients as well as to benefit themselves from the synergy between the two markets. Most participants acknowledge that their Euro-bond activity is a service function and rarely provides a significant profit after all overhead costs are taken into consideration. In several cases it is clear that a parent bank places a high priority on participation, regardless of profitability, in the Euro-bond market through its offspring. As in the case of Euro-currency tombstones, the satisfaction of seeing one's subsidiary listed as an underwriter is a major motivation for many parent banks. On the other hand, many banks engaged in all facets of Euro-bond activity regard the business as extremely profitable and express the view that such a comprehensive approach is the only one which ensures profitability.

Sharply different views exist on the merits of maintaining a secondary trading market in a specific number of outstanding issues. At least two of the banks in the sample suffered highly publicised and substantial book losses on their dealing portfolio which went some way towards offsetting banking profits in the year the loss was taken. On the other hand, other banks have achieved regular profits from their trading portfolio in good as well as bad years, which they attribute to being willing and able to cut back their portfolio on short notice. Negative carry margins in periods of high interest rates as in 1974 and 1978 have significantly eroded the profitability of the overall securities function of all banks.

Placing power is universally regarded as the key ingredient without which a Euro-bond operation is seriously prejudiced both in terms of vulnerability to adverse price movements and ability to gain admittance to underwriting syndicates. In developing their placing power, Euro-banks have solicited the traditional large takers of bonds such as the major Swiss banks as well as attempted to cultivate their own placing power, often with customers of the parent banks who had not previously been active as takers of Euro-bonds. Parent banks who manage international portfolios have been of significant assistance in many cases to their Euro-bank affiliates by taking a good portion, if not all, of their allocation. In a few cases, Euro-banks themselves manage international portfolios which provide useful placing power.

Even if a bank develops its own placing capability and manages to avoid portfolio losses by rigidly controlling the size of its trading portfolio, it is recognised that the most attractive profits in the Euro-bond business are derived from business origination. This sector, however, has traditionally been dominated by the major Wall Street investment banks, UK merchant banks and the principal continental mixed banks. To the extent that these institutions have an equity interest in a Euro-bank, some of the benefits may flow through to the latter in the form of a co-managership or underwriting group membership, but in many other instances, the Euro-bank has actually been excluded from Euro-bond activity because of the presumed duplication of effort with the parent this might involve. The ties between investment banks and their clients have traditionally been strong, and the Euro-banks have not been able to penetrate this market through their lending muscle as they have in the Euro-currency sector. Even the Euro-banks owned by the very largest American commercial banks have only made limited inroads into the lead management preserve of the traditional investment banking institutions in the US and Europe even where their parent institutions play a major role in the target customer's commercial banking picture. Even where a lead managership can be obtained, the pressures to share the management fee with a growing number of other institutions have substantially reduced the profitability of origination.

In explaining their reasoning, the roughly equal number of Euro-banks which have eschewed the Euro-bond sector generally point to the difficulty of developing placing power in competition with several hundred other placers all marketing the same merchandise to a restricted number of takers. They are only too conscious of the impact on their profit and loss statement of a book portfolio loss suffered if interest rates turn unexpectedly upward. For a Euro-bank attempting to keep personnel and overhead costs to a minimum, the need to hire bond salesmen, dealers and administrative staff represents a significant incremental overhead which may or may not be justified by the eventual results. As a practical compromise with the objectives of their stockholders and their own understandable desire to appear as a co-manager or participant, several Euro-banks have participated passively in a handful of issues brought out by major clients of their parent banks without setting up a full-fledged Euro-bond department.

Although a few of the active participants in the Euro-bond market were pleased with the profit performance of this activity over a reasonable period of time, the great majority expressed disappointment at the average level of profitability. As in the case of the loan syndication market, an influx of entrants attracted by the prestige of the securities business has depressed profitability for all participants, to which are added the periodic losses inherent in funding a bond portfolio at a cost significantly in excess of current yields.

A third general area of income generation is corporate financial services, which include a wide range of fee-earning activities: investment management; arranging back-to-back loans; project financing; leasing; new issues; mergers and acquisitions; private placements of fixed interest obligations; export financing; and advice on fund raising and corporate restructuring. The investment or merchant banking vocation of many Euro-bankers, coupled with the obvious attractions of earning possibly substantial fees without burdening the balance sheet, have led many Euro-banks to undertake some sort of corporate finance activity. Whereas in 1975 only about half of the banks interviewed either had established a formal corporate finance function or had engaged informally in some type of financial service activity, by 1979 all but a handful of the forty institutions had developed a capability which had resulted in the booking of at least a few non-asset related fees. In a number of cases, a large corporate finance staff had been recruited and a major priority placed on specialties such as project advisory work, investment management, private placements and back-to-back loans.

In setting up this activity, the banks have naturally focused on their functional and geographical strengths. Some banks with stockholders in the major world exporting countries have developed multinational export finance capabilities which enable the bank to put together extremely complex, multicurrency financing packages for their clients based on utilisation of the national export credit facilities of the OECD nations. Banks with parents in countries with active national stock markets often sell a securities portfolio management capability to individuals and institutions with specialisation in these particular markets. In the same vein, a bank with strong regional connections usually offers a merger and acquisition service focusing on that specific region. Banks with energy expertise have put together major offshore oil field financings, arranged the sale of oil-producing properties and advised customers on acquisition of North Sea acreage.

A number of Euro-banks which currently have only a limited corporate finance capability acknowledged that their institution must focus more on this type of fee-earning skill in the future even though they had not yet determined how to attack the problem. Behind this view lies not only the prospect of attractive profits but also a growing awareness of the need to differentiate themselves from other Euro-banks as well as the activities of those stockholders who are becoming increasingly active directly in the Euro-currency market.

Success in the corporate finance sector for most Euro-banks to date has been relatively modest in terms both of profits and tangible results. A number of Euro-banks have successfully put together mergers and acquisitions for a fee, quite a number of complex projects have been structured, and investment management for a few banks probably produces reasonable profits. Of the institutions which had some form of corporate finance activity in 1979, only a minority appeared to be more than covering their overhead in this sector. On balance, few chief executives indicated that corporate finance was now or likely in the near future to become a significant profit centre. In attempting to attract this business, Euro-banks are competing with national investment, merchant and mixed banks who have long-standing and successful relationships with the corporate clients who are the logical candidates for their service. The success ratio of any merger-acquisition or project finance team is traditionally quite low in view of the number of obstacles to be cleared and the time and effort usually required to bring a deal to fruition. Perhaps equally important is the personal factor: a successful corporate finance executive is extremely well compensated and is naturally inclined to stay with a prestigious firm with a good reputation for corporate finance; attracting such an individual to an organisation with a predominantly banking orientation and compensation structure is a major task.

Another source of profits for a limited number of Euro-banks is the provision of such traditional commercial banking services as documentary credit financing and the operation of correspondent banking clearing accounts. These relatively labour-intensive activities have been avoided by most Euro-banks who consider themselves wholesale banks with a limited client base, but the experience of several banks indicates that these more traditional activities can produce a useful profit.

The final and perhaps most controversial activity of Euro-banks is the taking of equity stakes either on an outright basis or in the form of a sweetener or kicker to a loan. As indicated in Chapter 1, merchant banking historically has involved the investment of a portion of bank's capital in trade and industry as well as providing the basis for lending business. By taking outright positions in commodities and project investments, banks like the Medici, Fugger, Barings and Rothschild probably produced useful trading profits to supplement their banking income. While the term 'merchant bank' is used rather loosely in the London market to cover anything from a pure Euro-currency lending bank to an aggressive institution with a major share of its assets in equities and high risk loans, a few Euro-banks in the early 1970s did invest in quoted and unquoted UK and foreign securities and made loans which were acknowledged to carry a level of risk with which a commercial bank might feel uncomfortable. While the world's stock and real estate markets were buoyant, significant profits were made on security gains and the realisation of equity kickers where the Euro-bank had invested seed money or provided a tranche of subordinated debt. The downturn in the markets in 1974, coupled with the interbank crisis of confidence in the same year, reinforced each other in bringing management and stockholders to the tentative conclusion that taking substantial amounts of equity-type risks and funding one's assets almost entirely in the interbank market might be inconsistent.

Despite these events, a small number of Euro-bank chief executives feel able to justify a strategy which included the taking of a selected number of equity kickers in conjunction with their basic banking business. While most Euro-banks feel that obtaining an equity swee-tener implies an unacceptable level of risk, a minority of bankers feel fully justified in asking for additional compensation in the form of a share in project earnings or residual value in connection with an extension of credit. Oil and shipping projects in the current market represent the principal vehicles for these sweeteners. In one case, a Euro-bank put together an oilfield financing which provided a percentage royalty to all lenders in addition to the usual interest compensation. Several banks lend to shipowners who provide such kickers as a share in profits, residual value or charter revenues as an inducement to make available terms, such as 100 per cent finance or lending on unchartered vessels, which do not fit standard commercial banking practice. Banks active in taking such sweeteners have found that only a relatively small number of these projects ever produce significant earnings to the bank and that the level of risk in retrospect often is greater than the lender had anticipated. On the other hand, the relatively exciting potential profits from this business continue to attract a limited number of banks interested in reinforcing their lending income and building on their specialist expertise.

6 Financial Performance

The financial performance of Euro-banks can perhaps best be evaluated by analysis of the published data of as large as possible a sample of Euro-banks for the period 1973–8. There exists precious little in the form of official compilations of this data or private surveys of institutions which correspond to my definition of Euro-banks. To provide comparable data for banks in different markets and, more importantly, to develop a sufficiently long time scale for comparative purposes, I have prepared my own Euro-bank samples for London, Hong Kong, Singapore and Luxembourg. Prior to 1973 the limited numbers and maturity of Euro-banks even in London render the data base of minimum utility to the analyst. The early years of the 1973–8 period, however, were quite significant in view of the credit losses incurred during 1974/75 and the liquidity problems stemming from the Herstatt crisis of confidence.

In selecting markets as well as individual banks for this chapter's analytical base, a number of arbitrary distinctions have been necessary. When the first edition of this volume was prepared in 1975, it was my view that only the London market provided a sufficiently large number of Euro-banks with a long enough financial track record to be useful for analytical purposes. A statistical sample of forty such banks was thus prepared and updated in 1979 for this edition. Each of these is authorised by the Bank of England and is either a UK–incorporated international bank or derives the major portion of its earnings from the Euro-markets through a London operating presence. The list of forty banks, with two exceptions, is identical to that of the sample banks interviewed. Smaller samples of eight banks each have been prepared for Luxembourg, Hong Kong and Singapore, each of which is the operating base for a relatively significant number of Euro-banks. In view of the relative youth of these markets and the Euro-banks located in them, statistical series have been somewhat shortened. Data for the period 1975–8 are included for the Hong Kong and Singapore samples, while only the 1976–8 period was felt to provide a sufficiently broad–based sample for Luxembourg. Other possible choices such as Paris were not covered in view of the relatively small number of Euro-banks located in these markets. Institutions making up the samples are listed in Appendix 1 on page 45.

These different financial centres have been analysed more to perceive trends within the given marketplace than to provide comparisons between centres. For a variety of reasons, such comparisons have limited usefulness. Local regulatory authorities establish their own guidelines for key ratios such as leverage (gearing); tax rates, accounting and reporting procedures differ radically, and each financial centre has a somewhat different profile of business. On the other hand, the Eurocurrency deposit and lending market is a world-wide one, and if one makes proper allowance for the different environmental factors, some tentative performance comparisons can be made between markets.

Selecting individual banks for each sample is even more difficult. Within the Eurobank definition of a separately capitalised institution deriving most, if not all, of its revenues from the Euro-markets, are banks which range from those operating totally independently of their stockholders to those which are in effect proxies for branches. The latter category, which is prevalent in Luxembourg and to a lesser extent Hong Kong, are utilised rather than branches by large national banks in given market centres for tax or regulatory reasons. They tend to be more highly leveraged, rely more on group sources for funding and assets, and have a relatively restricted lending authority compared with Euro-banks at the other end of the spectrum. In selecting banks for the four samples, an effort has been made to emphasise Euro-banks which operate with relative independence from their parents and therefore can be regarded as prototype international banks rather than specialised appendages of one or more large national institutions. However, to provide a sufficiently broad sample and to reflect the fact that 'independence' can only be relative when ownership is largely in the hands of other banks, the samples inevitably include Euro-banks which are situated throughout the spectrum. While a total of forty banks makes up the London sample, however, it was felt that the smaller number of relatively mature Euro-banks in the three other centres could only justify a sample of eight banks in each market.

In structuring the sample, an effort has been made to include institutions whose age, size, sponsorship, range of activities and financial performance is reasonably representative of the Euro-bank sector as a whole. A number of caveats should be borne in mind in evaluating these figures.

With regard, for example, to the London sample, banking disclosure under UK law is limited in a number of significant aspects. Published balance sheet and income statement detail is quite rudimentary. Banks are permitted to make undisclosed allocations to loss reserves, which may be taxed or not depending on the UK Inland Revenue's views as to whether a loss reserve can be justified by a specific likely loss, and a number of banks have established significant undisclosed reserves of both categories.

As was pointed out in Chapter 3, radically different management philosophies regarding loss reserve allocations are reflected in reported data for individual banks. Such key items as fee income and deferred tax are accounted for differently by London-based Euro-banks. Some banks book fee income when a loan is completed, while others amortise this income over the life of the loan. In recent years in line with British accounting recommendations, some Euro-banks have taken a portion of their deferred tax reserve into income. Extremely little detail is given in individual financial statements; a breakdown of income and expense items is rarely available, and the key categories of loans and deposits are usually given as one line items with at most a breakdown between loans maturing in less than and over one year. While cash in bank and call or short-date loans are broken out as a one-line item, liquidity analysis is often hampered by the lumping together of other liquid assets with loans to banks of up to one year in maturity.

Similar limitations apply to reported data used in the other samples. In addition, Luxembourg banks do not break out income taxes paid, while the relatively low or nonexistent taxes paid by Hong Kong and Singapore banks obviously limit the value of after-tax performance comparisons with London banks. Finally, the reported data of wholly-owned subsidiaries can clearly be manipulated by the sale of bad loans to the parent, the contribution of new business as well as under-priced resources and the booking of fees which arguably could be attributed to other elements of the group. On the basis of the publicly available information, however, Euro-bank financial performance can be analysed in terms of several key relationships:

(1) gearing (leverage) as measured by the ratios of deposits to capital funds and customer loans to capital funds. These data are given in Tables J and K for the sample banks. While more sophisticated techniques of leverage analysis exist, and the Bank of England as indicated previously has begun to refine the definition of 'stockholder funds', these ratios give a rough approximation of Euro-bank gearing.

(2) customer loans to deposits as an indication of the extent to which deposits are used to fund customer or interbank loans. Tables L and

M provide this data for the period ended 1978.
(3) liquid assets as a percentage of deposits, as shown in Tables N and O, give some indication of the short term liquid resources available to meet a deposit run off.
(4) profitability as measured by pre-tax profits as a percentage of stockholder funds and net income as a percentage of net assets is indicated in Tables P and Q. The pre-tax relationship excludes the variable of differential tax rates, while the net profits indicator represents a useful comparison in view of the wide range of individual gearing ratios.

In Tables J through Q the following definitions are used:

Deposits include C/Ds or other obligations issued and may include a small amount of other liabilities if not broken out.
Stockholder funds include all subordinated debt provided by stockholders and, in a few cases, outside investors.
Customer loans include loans to local authorities and bills of exchange if broken out separately.
Liquid assets include cash and due from banks and discount houses (for periods of up to one month depending on auditing procedure), C/Ds (if broken out) and short-term liquid government securities (if broken out). Because of the significant variations in reporting practice, only tentative conclusions can be drawn from these data.
Pre-tax income includes interest paid on stockholder subordinated debt if provided separately but is net of additions to loan loss reserves apparently relating to that year.
Net income is taken before formation expenses, additions to contingency reserves which do not apparently relate to that year, and other extraordinary items.
Average stockholder funds and total assets are derived, for the purpose of simplicity in calculation, by dividing the sum of the beginning and end year figures by two. In some cases, year end data are used for the earliest period in view of limitations on data sources.
Year end is approximately 31 December; latest statement available is used, although no statement for a period ending subsequent to 30 June 1979 has been used. For banks completing their first full year of operations, period covered can range up to seventeen months.
Banks selected are listed in Appendix I and include for the London sample authorised Euro-banks which are primarily UK companies but also include foreign Euro-banks whose London branches repre-

sent a major portion of total earnings and assets. Given the wide divergence around the average figures cited in each table for the London sample, the ranges of top and bottom quartiles are also provided.

As indicated in Chapter 4, the level of gearing varies widely among Euro-banks and is clearly a key factor in evaluating performance. A variety of considerations determine management or stockholders' attitude toward gearing; these include the ability to attract incremental deposits from the market, evaluation of the risk component of a given loan portfolio, the views of the local regulatory authorities, and of course the desire to maximise profits.

TABLE J   *Gearing (Leverage) Ratios for London Euro-Bank Sample*

Year ended approx. 12/31	Deposits as Multiple of Stockholder Funds			Customer Loans as Multiple of Stockholder Funds		
	Average	*Top Quartile*	*Bottom Quartile*	*Average*	*Top Quartile*	*Bottom Quartile*
1973	16.7	19.5–32.8	.6–12.7	7.9	9.8–26.6	3.1–4.3
1974	13.8	17.9–30.6	2.9–10.3	7.6	10.0–20.6	.8–4.4
1975	14.0	17.0–26.7	3.7–10.1	8.2	9.7–21.3	1.8–5.6
1976	15.8	19.0–24.1	4.1–12.8	9.5	12.0–21.7	1.5–6.0
1977	15.5	18.3–25.0	5.5–12.6	9.1	11.0–18.9	2.0–6.7
1978	15.2	17.5–27.7	4.8–12.4	9.3	11.2–19.9	1.4–6.7

Tables J and K provide gearing ratios for the period ended 1978 for London-based Euro-banks and institutions based in the other three financial centres respectively. Whereas the average deposits: capital funds ratio has traditionally provided the most useful measure of bank leverage, the wide variations in the proportion of relatively riskless interbank deposits justifies the use of the customer loans : stockholder funds ratio which provides a better measure of asset risk as well as a superior criterion for evaluating profitability in view of the low return on interbank assets.

Over the 1973–8 period, the London banks have shown no particular trend in the average deposits: stockholder funds ratio which has fluctuated between 14 : 1 and 16 : 1. There has, however, been a marginal upward trend in the customer loans : stockholder funds ratio, which has

TABLE K   *Average Gearing (Leverage) Ratios for non-London Euro-Bank Samples at Year-end*

Year ended approx. 12/31	Deposits as Multiple of Stockholder Funds	Customer Loans as Multiple of Stockholder Funds
	HONG KONG	
1975	8.5	6.0
1976	9.4	6.3
1977	9.4	6.3
1978	11.0	7.0
	SINGAPORE	
1975	11.8	10.5
1976	11.3	10.4
1977	12.1	10.8
1978	11.5	9.3
	LUXEMBOURG	
1976	25.3	13.6
1977	27.3	15.4
1978	28.7	15.7

risen from roughly 7 : 1 in 1973/74 to 9 : 1 in the 1976/78 period. This phenomenon is probably attributable to a desire to reduce the proportion of interbank loans in the face of conflicting pressures to increase profitability yet maintain or reduce gearing.

During the six-year period, the dispersion of individual gearing ratios around the average, while remaining quite wide, narrowed considerably. The more highly-geared banks have come under pressure from the Bank of England as well as market and stockholder forces to reduce their leverage, while the newer banks on the other hand increased their gearing as they built up their books of business. Whereas the high and low deposit : stockholder funds ratios in 1973 were 32.8 : 1 and .6 : 1 respectively, the comparable 1978 numbers were 27.7 : 1 and 4.8 : 1.

While the newer banks tend to be less highly geared than most, there is no particular correlation between number of years of operation and level of gearing. A much higher degree of correlation exists between physical size and gearing. In 1978, for example, the five banks with total assets exceeding £500 million had an average gearing of 18.0:1 while the five with assets under £100 million showed one of 8.4:1. Banks with the lowest levels of gearing tend to be smaller institutions and those active primarily in the securities rather than the Euro-currency market, while those with higher leverage are generally the larger institutions and those playing a specialist role in building assets for their stockholders.

The data for Hong Kong, Singapore and Luxembourg banks shown in Table K also reflect relatively stable gearing ratios within each market. The Hong Kong deposits: stockholder funds ratio has risen somewhat to a level of 11:1 in 1978, while the comparable range for Singapore is 11–12:1 and for Luxembourg 25–29:1. As in the case of the London sample, it is the largest Euro-banks—generally the subsidiaries or affiliates of very substantial national banks who utilise the Euro-bank as a substitute for a branch—who have the highest absolute levels of leverage, while the smaller institutions, often with relatively small parent banks, generally show the lowest gearing. The relatively high gearing shown by the Luxembourg sample reflects the use of this financial centre by German and Scandinavian institutions as a booking centre for their Euro-currency business; for regulatory and other reasons, separately capitalised Euro-bank subsidiaries rather than branches are used. Once again, the relatively constant average levels of gearing mask contrary individual movements as new banks build up their leverage while others gear down because of the declining attractiveness of lending opportunities, transfer of business to other centres, and regulatory pressures.

Another critical variable is the asset breakdown between customer loans and other assets, primarily interbank loans, as reflected in the ratio of customer loans to total deposits. As indicated earlier in Chapter 3, attitudes toward the composition of a Euro-bank's asset breakdown reflect such considerations as the desire to be seen as a significant lender as well as taker in the interbank market, the objective of maximisation of profits, the extent of attractive customer lending opportunities and attitudes towards liquidity management. Tables L and M provide loan:deposit ratios for the sample banks.

For the London sample analysed in Table L, the average loan : deposit ratio has reached a plateau of around 60 per cent following a sharp increase in the 1973–5 period. While they have narrowed somewhat in recent years, wide variations around the norm still exist; in 1978 individual ratios ranged from 20 per cent to 89 per cent. The banks at the high end of the scale are relatively inactive in the interbank market as lenders and generally expressed the view that redeposits in this market

TABLE L   *Customer Loans as Percentage of Deposits for London Euro-Bank Sample*

Year ended approx. 12/31	Average	Top Quartile	Bottom Quartile
1973	50	62–92	12–30
1974	59	76–102	9–44
1975	61	79–92	7–45
1976	61	71–99	6–49
1977	60	74–90	26–45
1978	61	75–89	20–51

represented a relatively low priority compared with profit maximisation. On the other hand, banks with relatively low loan : deposit ratios included those making a conscious effort for liquidity and relationship purposes and to relend a high proportion of interbank deposits, banks whose priority role was to place surplus liquidity from their stockholders, and institutions which were primarily active in the Euro-bond markets.

The non-London samples summarised in Table M show a similar rise in loan : deposit ratios since the mid-1970s as the pressure to increase earnings and the branch proxy role of many Euro-banks has more than offset the desire to show a balance in asset mix. While Luxembourg ratios have tended in recent years to approximate those of London banks, in Singapore substantially higher loan : deposit ratios in the region of 85–95 per cent prevail.

One of the most difficult relationships to analyse from published information is that of individual bank liquidity. While the Bank of England data on maturity mismatch shown in Chapter 4 provides a most useful indication of trends and levels of liquidity for different categories of banks, the lack of detail in individual balance sheets for key short-term asset and liability items places real limitations on the conclusions which can be drawn from any statistical analysis. Assuming that assets available as a liquidity cushion include cash in bank, call loans to the money market, short term interbank deposits, certificates of deposit and other prime marketable, short-term obligations, it is possible in the case of most Euro-banks to compute the relationship between these assets and total deposits as a rough measure of the bank's ability to realise assets to cover a liquidity gap.

While useful, it must also be borne in mind that any liquidity ratio is taken at the fiscal year end when window dressing – usually through

TABLE M   *Customer Loans as Percentage of Deposits for non-London Euro-Bank Sample*

Year ended approx. 12/31	Amount
HONG KONG	
1975	65
1976	67
1977	69
1978	64
SINGAPORE	
1975	87
1976	96
1977	93
1978	89
LUXEMBOURG	
1976	56
1977	58
1978	55

matching short date interbank transactions – may camouflage a more normal liquidity ratio. Most importantly, only a running measure of a Euro-bank's overall mismatch position on a maturity basis as calculated by the Bank of England can truly reflect the day to day vulnerability of a Euro-bank to a crisis in which it could not renew its deposit liabilities. Needless to say, such data are not readily available.

In measuring a Euro-bank's liquidity exposure, the Bank of England would appear to relate a bank's standby lines of credit from stockholders and the market and its realisable short term assets to an arbitrary time period of several weeks or more which would give the bank, its stockholders and perhaps appropriate regulatory authorities sufficient time to work out a longer term solution to a liquidity crisis. As indicated by the nature of the 1974 crisis of confidence, traditional methods of liquidity measurement became somewhat less relevant in a market environment where a bank's presumed or actual difficulties can result in its name becoming unacceptable in the market within days with the resulting virtual impossibility of rolling over any of its interbank liabilities.

TABLE N   *Liquid Assets as Percentage of Deposits of London Euro-Bank Sample*

Year ended approx. 12/31	Average	Top Quartile	Bottom Quartile
1973	29	35–80	5–18
1974	29	43–82	1–16
1975	29	39–79	2–15
1976	26	35–68	1–17
1977	25	30–58	3–19
1978	25	27–69	0–16

Table N provides an analysis for the period ended 1978 of the proportion of deposits held by the London sample banks in liquid assets. As the asset breakdowns published for individual banks are fragmentary and not always comparable, only limited conclusions can be drawn from the available data.

From Table N, the apparent steady decline in liquidity of the typical London Euro-bank since the 1973–5 period is clearly demonstrated. From roughly 28–9 per cent in these years, the ratio has steadily declined to 25 per cent in 1978. Behind this decline lie such factors as the increasing pressure to maximise return on assets, the build-up of customer loan portfolios at the expense of liquid resources, and in many cases a determination (often as a result of a stockholder change) to rely on parent institutions for liquidity.

The most striking aspect of Table N is the extreme variations around the mean liquidity ratio. Throughout the 1973–8 period individual banks have reported 1 per cent or less of their deposits in liquid assets, while for others ratios have reached the low 80s. On the other hand, the quartile ranges for the most liquid banks have dropped steadily over the period from 43–82 per cent in 1974 to 27–69 per cent in 1978. Even allowing for the limited comparability of data, such a range seems to reflect totally disparate philosophies of asset and liability management.

Table O provides comparable data for sample banks in the three other financial centres. The same downward trend is reflected in all three samples, with each indicating a relatively lower degree of liquidity than the London banks. The Singapore sample average has dropped from 25 per cent in 1975 to virtually zero in 1978, while a similar sharp reduction from 29 per cent in 1975 is indicated by the Hong Kong sample.

Institutions with low liquidity tend to be banks who suffered acknowledged funding problems during the period as well as those, both

TABLE O   *Liquid Assets as Percentage of Deposits for non-London Bank Samples*

Year Ended Approx. 12/31	Amount
HONG KONG	
1975	29
1976	16
1977	8
1978	6
SINGAPORE	
1975	25
1976	6
1977	9
1978	1
LUXEMBOURG	
1976	15
1977	12
1978	11

consortium banks and wholly owned subsidiaries, who consider that their stockholders provide a sufficient liquidity backstop and believe that their primary objective is to run a customer loan portfolio rather than participate actively as a lender in the interbank market. Several banks with particularly high liquidity ratios are traditionally active as net lenders in the interbank market of funds derived from stockholders. A number of the relatively liquid institutions are those primarily active in the securities markets. There is no particular correlation between size of bank and liquidity. In many cases, of course, year end ratios are far from typical of experience during the year because of the desire on the part of many banks to show a high proportion of presumably liquid assets on their balance sheet date.

Profitability is acknowledged by most senior Euro-bank management to be one of the principal objectives of their organisation. A number of these individuals point also to non-quantifiable objectives which may be equally or more important, such as obtaining an exposure to the Euro-markets, working together with a compatible group of banks, or providing a service not otherwise available to customers of the parent institutions.

A fairly significant minority of the executives interviewed felt, however, that setting a profitability target was either impractical or irrelevant to the needs of the stockholders. Several executives expressed the view that their realised return on invested funds was dependent on market and other forces, such as the Bank of England, which were beyond their control. Since these banks could not control such vital variables as spread and maturities (set by market forces) and gearing (set by market forces or the Bank of England), establishing a fixed percentage return could, in the view of some managers, result in an arbitrary and possibly dangerous target. Much better, in their view, would be to evaluate all Euro-banks on a relative performance basis. A number of other chief executives, in particular those heavily involved in the securities markets, felt that the volatility of earnings in this sector was such that any profit target for year-to-year performance was totally unrealistic.

For those prepared to cite a given criterion which they considered to be the appropriate measure of their performance, the majority mentioned return on stockholder funds. A minority preferred return on assets as the relevant criterion, while still others use both measures. A few banks have established as their sole profit goal the steady annual absolute increase in reported earnings.

A particular problem in establishing profit criteria occurs for a number of American-owned Euro-banks functioning as flagship merchant banks in that they form part of a global functional sector—merchant or investment banking—within their group's matrix structure. While earnings levels can be established internally for that particular function, the profitability within this function of a capitalised vehicle, which may or may not carry a significant loan portfolio, is a secondary, almost irrelevant consideration. Moreover, it is recognised by these banks that their earnings in this context should be split between those derived from commercial banking—free capital funds and the leverage provided by a loan portfolio—and those from investment banking which do not relate to a given capital or asset base. A number of US-owned banks are thus wrestling with such issues as the appropriate size of their capital base and the remuneration this capital should receive.

For the great majority of Euro-bankers who expressed a view on a reasonable long-term earnings objective for their bank, the percentage returns (after 52 per cent UK corporation tax) indicated range from $7\frac{1}{2}$ per cent to 20 per cent after tax on total stockholders' funds. The figure most often cited ranged from 10 per cent to 15 per cent after tax. In many cases, management felt an implicit or explicit pressure from their stockholders to exceed the return on capital achieved by the stockholders in their own banking businesses. Implicit in these targets is the gearing ratio they judged reasonable, which was discussed in more detail in Chapter 4. For the minority which utilise return on assets as a key profit criterion, an after-tax ratio of .75 per cent to 1 per cent on total assets is usually expressed as the objective.

Some interesting trends emerged from a comparison of the interview results between 1975 and 1979. While a few Euro-banks had adjusted their profitability target upwards between the two interviews, a much larger number had either lowered them, determined that the target should be achieved on average or over an extended number of years, or actually discontinued the practice of setting specific targets. In most cases the change in approach reflected actual results achieved (both above and below target) during the period as management has come to grips with its ability to perform in the competitive marketplace.

Table P presents data for the London sample for two measurements of profitability: pre-tax return on stockholder funds and net income as a percentage of total assets. The former reflects the traditional return on equity calculation; income is taken before tax to eliminate the impact of differential tax rates and before deduction of interest paid on stockholder subordinated debt in their capital structure. The measure of net income as a percentage of net assets is used primarily because of the wide variations in bank gearing which, if profitability is measured as return on stockholder funds, places the less highly geared banks at an obvious disadvantage. For both calculations, average stockholder funds and net assets are used as the denominator because of the frequency of sharp increases in these figures during the year. Earnings for several banks in

TABLE P   *Profitability calculations for Sample of London Euro-banks*

Year Ended approx. 12/31	Pre-tax Income as % of Average Stockholder Funds			Net Income as % of Average Total Assets		
	%	Top Quartile	Bottom Quartile	%	Top Quartile	Bottom Quartile
1973	12.8	16.3–39.5	3.3 – 7.5	.32	.35–1.08	.05 –.20
1974	14.1	18.3–53.6	loss– 6.6	.33	.43– .79	loss–.08
1975	15.7	21.2–40.8	loss– 8.2	.46	.60–1.20	loss–.22
1976	21.5	26.9–91.5	1.6 –13.1	.61	.80–2.36	.05 –.30
1977	18.9	23.9–69.7	loss–11.4	.54	.76–2.97	loss–.26
1978	18.8	25.5–53.5	loss–11.8	.58	.79–1.55	.06 –.33

Note: Banks with loss results excluded from calculations for years in which loss occurred the sample are undoubtedly understated in view of the ability to transfer taxed or untaxed earnings on an undisclosed basis to hidden asset reserves.

In addition, different treatment of loan loss reserve allocations distorts the data as does the practice in recent years on the part of some banks of including part or all of this deferred tax reserve as income. Finally, a further distortion is provided by currency fluctuations in that UK-incorporated banks were able to invest their capital much more flexibly in terms of currency exposure than other institutions. Some of these latter chose to retain the bulk of their capital in their parent's currency as a hedge against the decline of sterling, while others took advantage of higher sterling interest rates and remained invested in sterling. The sharp decline in sterling through 1976 and its subsequent recovery thus had a major differential impact on London-based banks' earnings. On the other hand, the pressure in most cases to report the maximum possible level of earnings for image and stockholder purposes, and the size of the sample should produce some reasonably valid results. In both pre-tax and after-tax terms, relative London Euro-bank profitability appears to have reached a plateau in the 1976–8 period after rising from the 1973–4 level. From a 13–14 per cent pre-tax return in the latter period, average yields on stockholder funds have moved in the 19–22 per cent bracket during the years 1976–8. In terms of return on assets, average net income as a percentage of total assets rose from the .32–.33 per cent level in 1973/74 to .54–.61 per cent during the last three years under analysis.

The improvement stems in large part from the maturation of a number of newer banks which had just been formed in the early 1970s as well as a profit recovery from the loan losses sustained by many Euro-banks in the 1974–5 period. Another factor affecting a large number of banks has been the ability of UK-incorporated banks to invest a major portion of their capital in currencies other than sterling; this flexibility could have resulted in large profits when sterling weakened in 1976 and equivalent losses in subsequent years. The rise in average loan spreads and the recovery in the bond markets clearly benefited Eurobank profits in 1975–6, while the accentuation of the borrowers market in 1977–8 significantly restrained the growth in earnings. The improvement in 1978 profitability is noteworthy in the face of declining lending margins, rising operating costs and declining bond prices, and would seem to indicate that Euro-banks have been able to develop sources of fee income as well as restrain the increase in expenses.

As was the case with the ratios previously discussed, wide variances

among individual banks have been shown throughout the period
analysed. Losses have been incurred by six sample banks during the
period, while individual returns on stockholder funds and total assets
have ranged up to 91.5 per cent and 2.97 per cent respectively.

Whereas in the 1973/74 period there was a high degree of correlation
between gearing and return on stockholder funds, this correlation was
no longer as valid in 1978. For example, in 1974 the fourteen banks with
customer loans of less than six times capital funds showed an average
pre-tax return on capital of only 7.6 per cent, with the highest in this
category achieving a 14 per cent return, while nine banks with ratios of
10:1 or more had an average return of 26.7 per cent. By 1978, however,
some of the least heavily geared institutions—primarily those with
significant fee and other investment banking earnings—showed extremely high returns on invested funds. For relatively ungeared banks
reliant on interest differential income, however, below average returns
continued to be realised. Thus, while the earnings impact of adding
loans on a given equity base is still important, the earning of fees and
other non-interest differential income obtained directly or through the
intervention of stockholder institutions has assumed greater significance
in recent years. The loss of income from non-performing problem loans
as well as additions to loan loss reserves has also reduced the correlation
of gearing and profitability.

The relative performance of individual banks over this period has
largely been a function of two factors—their ability to generate this non-
interest differential income and to minimise the earnings drain from
problem loans. The highest returns on equity and assets have been
earned by Euro-banks with a relatively significant proportion of income
from loan and bond management as well as corporate finance fees, in
particular the Euro-banks owned by large US institutions active in
Euro-currency loan syndications and the regional specialists who have
played a major role in initiating such transactions. The results of some of
the wholly-owned Euro-banks must, of course, be analysed in the light
of their parent's ability to transfer earnings within the group.

The poorest earnings, on the other hand, have invariably been the
product of loan losses and the loss of interest from non-performing
loans. Whereas no bank in the sample reported a loss in 1973, four were
in the red in 1974, two in 1975 and one in 1977. In most cases these losses
stemmed largely from property loans which went sour when the UK, US
and other property markets collapsed or dried up in 1974–5. A few
banks were hurt in 1974 and 1978 by the decline in bond prices, while
others which held equity securities for their own account suffered from

the collapse of stock markets around the world in the 1974–5 recession. Between these two extremes lies a number of Euro-banks essentially engaged in various commercial banking activities—trade finance, the participation in Euro-loans generated by others, and the running of a money or treasury function. While they are developing their customer base, the non-interest differential income which is derived from initiating a fee-earning transaction is not yet an important element of their earnings, and their profit results tend to be grouped around the average for the sample.

Other less visible factors which are not revealed in published data but may well have affected the results of individual banks are the level of dealing profits and of operating costs. With regard to the former, Euro-bankers are understandably reluctant to divulge a major loss on F/X dealing or deposit mismatch, but it can be assumed that the performance of individual bank dealing rooms has varied widely over a period when interest and exchange rates have fluctuated significantly. A Euro-bank which was well positioned in terms of mismatch book or took the correct view on major currencies could have significantly added to its overall results.

In terms of operating expenses, which are published by only a very few Euro-banks, one can equally assume that there are large variations among banks in terms of profit/productivity per employee and cost of premises. The cost of space in the City of London has moved considerably over the years, and a bank fortunate enough to avoid paying the top levels charged in 1972–3 could achieve a significant cost saving over a competitor. For individual high overhead functions such as corporate finance, the management of Euro-bond issues and trade finance, profitability can vary widely depending on the ability to generate business which covers this expensive overhead.

Finally, in recent years non-operating or accounting decisions have probably had a major impact on the results of individual banks. As mentioned previously, UK-incorporated banks were permitted by the Bank of England to deploy a major portion of their capital in non-sterling currencies; for banks which took advantage of this flexibility, the 1976–77 period could have reflected large F/X gains or losses as a result of the sharp fall and subsequent rise of sterling. Reported results have also been affected by the decision on the part of many banks to establish general as well as specific loss reserves from pre-tax income. Finally, some Euro-banks decided in 1978 to take advantage of new accounting guidelines to incorporate part or all of their accumulated deferred tax into current earnings.

TABLE Q   *Profitability Calculation for Samples of Non-London Euro-Banks*

Year ended approx. 12/31	Pre-Tax Income as % of Average Stockholder Funds	Net income as % of Total Assets
	HONG KONG	
1975	19.0	1.35
1976	17.4	1.50
1977	15.7	1.26
1978	17.4	1.17
	SINGAPORE	
1975	21.2	1.10
1976	21.8	.94
1977	15.8	.99
1978	17.2	1.11
	LUXEMBOURG	
1976	NA	.41
1977	NA	.42
1978	NA	.42

Table Q provides similar profitability data for the Hong Kong, Singapore and Luxembourg samples. Given the relatively low or virtually non-existent effective levels of tax in Hong Kong and Singapore (Luxembourg banks do not break out the tax figures) a pre-tax comparison with London and other banks is the more relevant criterion.

Pre-tax returns on shareholder funds in both Hong Kong and Singapore have declined somewhat from the levels established in 1975. In the latter instance, the sample average dropped from 21.2 per cent in 1975 to 17.2 per cent in 1978. In recent years the samples in each of the two financial centres have produced roughly the same pre-tax returns, which have tended to be somewhat lower than the recent plateau achieved by the London sample.

Hong Kong and Singapore Euro-banks range from very small and lightly capitalised institutions to quite substantial institutions functioning largely as a branch substitute for one or more national banks. Some of the former are actively engaged in local capital market activities as well as Euro-currency lending. As in the case of London banks, loan write-offs have produced losses for several banks in the samples; in 1975 one sample bank in each centre operated in the red.

In general, however, it has been increased competition in the form of lower lending margins and more entrants into local capital markets which has been responsible for the decline in relative profitability over the 1975–8 period. During the mid-1970s, loan margins for many Far East borrowers were relatively high because of the perceived risk of several major sovereign borrowers; by 1977–8, however, the entrance of non-traditional lenders into these markets had brought spreads down to levels characteristic of European and other borrowers. Rising operating costs, in particular for expatriate personnel, have also played a role.

The best pre-tax results in the Singapore and Hong Kong samples have been generated by institutions with significant locally-based capital market or lending business derived from a local stockholder or through the bank's own business development efforts in speciality sectors such as shipping. Some of the poorest results, on the other hand, are products of loan losses stemming from local and non-local borrowers who collapsed in the world-wide 1974–5 recession. Average earnings have been reported by institutions essentially engaged in interest differential lending without a major portion of fee income.

On a net income basis, returns on total assets for the three samples have shown stable or slightly declining trends over the 1975–8 period. The superior performance of Hong Kong over Singapore banks reflects in large part the virtual absence of corporation tax in Hong Kong for the period analysed, whereas Singapore banks are subject to a 10 per cent tax on income derived from offshore transactions.

The net income data reported by Luxembourg banks is of marginal use to the analyst in view of the widespread practice of understating reported earnings. In addition to the obvious ability to transfer earnings to and from a wholly-owned Euro-bank affiliate through cost allocations and other practices, Luxembourg banks benefit from the ability to over-reserve for losses on bond and loan portfolios. The analyst might, therefore, assume that real earnings on assets are much closer to the London average than the .41–.42 per cent level actually reported in the 1975–8 period.

To compare the foregoing Euro-bank ratios with those of national banking institutions is at best a hazardous proposition. Differences in disclosure and accounting practices, regulatory and business environments, costs and tax rates—not to speak of the vast differences in size and maturity between the typical large national bank and the Euro-bank—necessarily limit the validity of the conclusions which can be drawn from such an analysis.

On the other hand, in a highly competitive banking industry which is becoming increasingly internationalised, the analytical value of Euro-banks as relatively pure, self-standing international banks is of sufficient importance to justify at least a rough comparison. Moreover, Euro-banks as a market phenomenon have reached a level of maturity where patterns of gearing, profitability and liquidity have become reasonably well established. Finally, and perhaps most relevant of all, it is these national banks which own most Euro-banks and, at least in the case of US and British institutions, will probably evaluate their Euro-bank affiliates' performance in terms of their own relative profitability.

In the absence of any recent, publicly available comparisons of key operating ratios, Table R has been prepared to contrast London Euro-bank operating ratios with those of sample national banks based in the US, the UK, Japan and key European countries. The years 1977 and 1978, the two most recent periods for which data are available, have been selected to provide a reasonably meaningful analytical base. Equity capital as a percentage of total assets has been used as a proxy for gearing, while relative profitability is measured by net income expressed both as a percentage of total assets and of stockholder funds. A fifty-bank sample of London-based Euro-banks prepared by IBCA Banking Analysis Limited is used, rather than the sample included in Appendix I, in order to provide comparable ratios with those calculated by IBCA for the national banks. Virtually all of the forty banks in Appendix I are included in the IBCA sample, however, and the average ratios of the two samples are sufficiently similar for analytical purposes (mean net income in 1978 as a percentage of average assets was .58 per cent for the forty banks and .57 per cent for the fifty institutions).

Table R indicates that Euro-banks are relatively conservatively geared in comparison with all but the UK sample. Euro-bank leverage in recent years of roughly 16 times capital funds has been roughly one-half that of Continental European and Japanese institutions and well below that of the larger US banks. Such conservative ratios of Euro-banks are understandable in view of the relatively small size of the typical London Euro-bank, the investment banking character of much of their business, and the institutional support behind most of the large national banks. The Euro-banks' lower gearing is also reflected in net return on stockholder funds; after tax average returns of 8–10 per cent in recent years have been well below the UK, US, Canadian and Dutch average but comparable with those reported by the more highly geared Japanese and German banks.

When the impact of differential leverage is substantially reduced by comparing yields on total assets, the Euro-bank average of .40–.60 per

TABLE R   *Comparison of London Euro-banks with Selected Banking Institutions in Key National Markets for years 1977 and 1978*

Bank Sample	Equity Capital as % of Total Assets		Net Income as % of Average Total Assets		Net Income as % of Average Stockholder Funds	
	1977	1978	1977	1978	1977	1978
50 London Euro-Banks*	5.76	6.05	.41	.57	8.34	9.96
United States: average of 22 banks with over $5 billion in assets	4.7	4.5	.52	.58	11.00	12.67
United Kingdom: average of 11 large commercial banks	6.0	6.3	.75	.81	13.30	13.67
West Germany: average of 9 universal banks	2.9	2.6	.27	.24	9.29	8.83
Canada: average of 4 major commercial banks	3.7	3.6	.58	.63	15.69	17.19
Holland: average of 5 large commercial banks	3.0	3.0	.40	.40	13.63	13.71
France: average of 8 large banks	2.3	2.9	.24	.23	11.27	9.19
Japan: average of 8 City Banks	3.5	3.0	.27	.25	7.54	7.34

Source: IBCA Banking Analysis Ltd. and Keefe Bruyette and Woods Inc.

* Includes virtually all of the banks in Appendix I plus a few other London-based consortium and merchant banks.

cent in recent years is comparable with US institutions, far superior to Japanese and most Continental European banks, and well below the levels achieved by British banks.

Perhaps the most valid conclusions to be drawn from an admittedly highly imperfect analysis of reported data can be derived from a comparison of Euro-bank data with that of the UK, US and Canadian institutions which use roughly comparable accounting conventions and place a high priority on return on assets and net worth as a management tool. The average Euro-bank has not achieved the levels of profitability shown by national banks in these countries, although clearly a large number of the former have shown results which are outstanding by any standard. One can only guess at the reasons for the differential performance; in all likelihood, the relative profitability of domestic banking with its base of inexpensive demand deposits and higher net interest margins contrasts with the highly competitive international market in which the Euro-banks operate.

7 Issues Arising from Euro-Bank Experience

In the period since the first Euro-banks appeared in the mid-1960s, an almost unprecedented physical growth in a boom atmosphere through 1973 was checked by a chain of psychological and economic shocks administered in 1974 by a series of bank failures, the prospect of substantial international loan losses for the first time since the Second World War, and the world-wide tremors created by the shift in resources to the OPEC countries. In the five years since this series of shocks, the Euro-banks have been confronted not only by increased competition in the international banking market which had drastically modified the risk/reward ratio in international lending, but also competition in a different sense from their stockholders which has forced them to re-examine their own objectives and strategy. Most Euro-banks have thus lived through periods of both boom and adversity, and, while many chapters in their history remain to be written, it is possible to identify in mid-1979 with greater precision the major unresolved issues confronted by these institutions.

With the wonderful gift of 20–20 hindsight, the Euro-boom which existed until early or mid-1974 was a unique mixture of real economic growth, the evolution of a new international financial market structure and a self-perpetuating optimism in this market in which growth and expanding profits were almost taken for granted. On the asset side of the balance sheet the more passive of the Euro-bankers could simply choose from the smörgasbord of syndicated offerings that arrived daily by telex on his desk, while the more aggressive could solicit business from a variety of borrowers throughout the world as well as develop the identity and expertise base which he felt was needed to differentiate his bank from his stockholders and other Euro-banks.

While new and untested borrowers appeared on their loan books, the outstanding post-war international loan loss record was maintained by steadily rising indices of business activity, increasing asset and stock market values, the willingness of new banks to take out existing lenders who were unhappy with the borrower, and amortisation schedules which did not particularly burden the early years of a credit. Increasing competition may have lowered loan spreads and lengthened maturities, but adding new loans had a positive impact in the short term on the profit and loss statement, especially if a front end fee could be booked when the loan went on the books.

On the liability side of the ledger, an often uncritical approach to the extension of interbank loans to new banks coupled with the rapid increase in the size of the interbank market meant that gearing levels could be increased significantly, availability of funds was often a secondary consideration, and there was little or no differentiation in the LIBOR rates paid by different banks. In this context there were few barriers to entry for a new Euro-bank. In London, Bank of England approval to deal in foreign currencies and deposits was granted to most banks sponsored by reputable banking institutions with at least several billion dollars of footings. Hiring key staff such as a competent chief dealer posed problems, but seconded personnel could often be used to set up the Euro-bank.

The events of 1974, however, produced in many respects the reverse of these boom conditions. Perhaps even more important than actual economic reality was the turnaround in market sentiment that at one point in the summer of 1974 threatened to jeopardise not only the viability of many Euro-banks but also the existence of the Euro-currency market itself. Loan spreads of $\frac{3}{4}$ per cent and less for maturities of ten years or more now in the cold light of balance sheet and funding constraints lost their attractiveness. The threat of a world-wide depression and several individual country balance of payments problems made Euro-banks take a second look at countries like Italy which heretofore had borrowed at the primest of rates. Specific sectors which previously had been at the forefront of economic progress and the chosen area of specialisation of many Euro-banks suddenly turned sour; property companies in the UK, American REITs and VLCC tankers without reliable charters threatened real or potential losses. Sovereign risk loans to countries in Latin America, Africa and Asia which could not possibly rank very highly on anyone's weighted average of country risk looked somewhat less attractive. Bankers became aware of the vulnerability of the quality of their country loans to the willingness of other banks to continue to lend to these countries and the widespread domino effect of one country's inability to meet its Euro-market obligations on the credit of similar countries. Like the Euro-banks themselves, many of their borrowers would no longer be viable if a steady if not increased current of bank financing were not forthcoming to meet current obligations.

The impact of the change in sentiment was perhaps even more devastating on the other side of the balance sheet. The failures of US National of San Diego, Herstatt and Franklin shattered any implicit assumptions that interbank loans to all market participants were virtually riskless.

The reaction of many major lenders in the interbank market was a cutting or reduction of interbank dealing lines to smaller and newer banks. Such a reaction came close to creating a self-fulfilling prophecy by which otherwise viable banks would, in fact, become unable to meet their obligations because of a desire on the part of lending banks to cut their exposure to presumably weaker institutions. In view of their relative newness and smaller size, many Euro-banks were forced to fall back on a combination of parent funding support, reduction of interbank lending activity, or, in a few cases, actual sale of assets to parent banks. By early 1975, however, action by central banks such as the Bank of England as well as the passage of time without the feared collapse of a number of Euro-banks brought about the restoration of many interbank lines, an increase in volume, and a generally more optimistic mood in the interbank market.

With both Euro and other banks – particularly American – increasingly conscious of the limitations on their ultimate gearing placed on them by regulatory authorities and the market, Euro-banks turned to a significantly revised risk/reward ratio in their lending policy as one of the few means by which long term profitability could be increased. In a change in market sentiment reminiscent of the post-Penn Central mood in 1970, banks re-established minimum lending spreads and maximum maturity periods at levels reflecting a new lender's market, and credit quality reassumed its primacy in bankers' thinking.

In the cold light of post-Herstatt dawn, management behaviour during the boom period must be analysed in psychological as well as economic terms. Psychologically, new institutions and new bankers felt an understandable desire to build a performance record. In a market of over 300 institutions with highly similar objectives and lending criteria, the knowledge that a competitor was after a piece of apparently desirable business seemed in many cases sufficient justification to make an offer 1/8 per cent lower in spread and a year longer in maturity. In a word, the herd instinct overcame legitimate concerns over risk/reward as bank after bank piled on a particular bandwagon. From an economic standpoint, pressures from stockholders and home offices to show increases in absolute earnings from Euro-dollar activities were reinforced by the good historical loss record since World War II and the apparent ease of making foreign exchange profits against fixed parities and mismatch profits by riding the yield curve. Return on capital was often regarded as a secondary consideration in the absence of pressure for a ceiling on leverage from regulatory authorities and the market itself.

In the five years since the 1974 crisis of confidence, international banking has seen a reaffirmation of the borrower's market which was interrupted in the 1974–5 period, with a corresponding increase in international lending capacity, a deterioration of the risk/reward ratio from the lender's standpoint and the proliferation of new banking entities established in financial centres throughout the world both by established international banks as well as newcomers who thereby reversed their more conservative, domestic-oriented strategies of the early 1970s. New standards of risk and reward established in the wake of the Herstatt crisis were gradually eroded by the personal and corporate imperatives to build and put to work an international infrastructure and show the profit growth promised when this infrastructure was initially committed. New branches, representative offices and subsidiaries were opened in relatively new financial centres such as Hong Kong, Singapore, Bahrain and various Caribbean islands; growing national markets such as Korea and the Philippines, as well as the traditional centres such as London and New York.

Another development of the late 1970s has been the growing importance of sovereign risk lending as well as the evidence, both positive and negative, of the ability and willingness of sovereign borrowers to meet their obligations. Whereas in 1975 it was argued by many that the prospect of loss of principal or interest on sovereign lending was minimal, the continued and open defaults on loans from commercial banks by such sovereign nations as Turkey and Zaire, together with the forced debt reschedulings negotiated by several others, has brought about a greater acceptance of the view that sovereign lending by commercial banks is not riskless and that prudent lenders should establish some form of general reserve to cover possible international losses.

Whereas the first half of the decade of the 1970s was characterised by the internationalisation of US and Canadian banks, during the latter half the North Americans were joined by European, Japanese and other banks which also adopted a universalist strategy of being able to do business in a wide variety of overseas financial markets as well as developing loan portfolios not necessarily related to their traditional domestic customers. Accompanying this increased capacity and pro-liferation of new offices has been an emphasis on broadening of product line to encompass both investment and commercial banking services. During the period it became apparent that the relative attractiveness of domestic banking opportunities has played a key role in the importance placed on international expansion; while European banks moved abroad to offset limited domestic expansion potential, the US regional banks were simultaneously withdrawing in favour of what were now regarded as more natural and profitable markets at home. As will be pointed out below, these movements have had major repercussions on the strategy and objectives of the Euro-banks themselves.

The principal objective of this chapter is to analyse the issues now faced by Euro-banks. A particular effort will be made to contrast the issues as perceived by the author in mid-1979 as opposed to mid-1975 when the first edition was written. To this end the 1979 interviews focused on Euro-bankers' own views of the issues which most concerned them. An effort has been made in the following analysis to focus on issues which relate primarily to Euro-banks as opposed to the Euro-currency market as a whole, although admittedly the distinction must be an arbitrary one. One such generic issue not discussed, for example, is Euro-currency loan pricing, which provides a theoretically assured gross margin but does not normally allow for such factors as changes in credit quality or the costs of doing business over a period of time which can exceed ten years.

One of the most fundamental issues confronted by Euro-banks is their relationship to their stockholders and the modification in strategy that is derived from a similar change at the parent level. This issue—which was not even noted by this author in 1975!—has surfaced in recent years in the form of major stockholder and strategy restructuring of Euro-banks attributable to parental initiatives rather than the specific situation of the Euro-bank itself. Of the forty Euro-banks comprising the London sample, ten went through major shifts in their ownership structure in the period between 1975 and 1979, while an equivalent number underwent a profound change in strategy either because of their new ownership or because of a different strategy adopted by the same stockholder. While some of these shifts were precipitated by major loan losses suffered by a management team which had been given a flexible brief by the stockholders, others were simply the product of a change in direction on the part of the parent itself.

The common thread running through most of these structural

changes is the increasing size, diversification and specialisation of the parent bank's international operations. Whereas in the late 1960s and early 1970s a relatively autonomous Euro-bank subsidiary or affiliate primarily engaged in Euro-currency lending did not pose any serious conflicts in the relatively small and unstructured international function of the parent, by the late 1970s considerable duplication of activity was perceived to exist as the latter developed an expanded and more sophisticated network. Equally important has been the declining attractiveness of interest differential lending and the corresponding importance placed on fee-earning activities which the Euro-bank affiliate is seen to be better equipped than another type of vehicle to pursue.

Whereas many Japanese and European-owned Euro-banks had already been designated at the outset as the group's investment or merchant banking vehicle, in the late 1970s most Euro-banks controlled by a major US bank were restructured to become a specialist vehicle with a regional or global investment banking brief. At one end of the spectrum are the American-owned Euro-banks which barely qualify for Bank of England authorised status in view of their limited dealing and lending activity but primarily exist to syndicate loans, run a Euro-bond book and carry on corporate finance activities. For these institutions, the cost of maintaining authorised status is often questioned internally in view of the limited benefits obtained. Some consortium banks were acquired by a single stockholder with this objective in mind, and others have been subjected to considerable stockholder pressure to develop non-lending activities which would complement rather than compete with the commercial banking operations of their stockholders.

While most Euro-bank managers recognise that such specialisation and focus on corporate finance or investment banking activities is highly desirable both to survive in a competitive market and to placate stockholders, they are also more than aware of the difficulties of attracting experienced staff, becoming comfortable with the risks involved in specialist finance, and penetrating the market dominated by traditional investment and universal banks.

When asked to cite the most difficult issue they confronted, five of the forty senior Euro-bankers interviewed in mid-1979 voiced their long term concern over how their institution could find a mutually acceptable role in the framework of the stockholders' objectives. The same issue was reflected indirectly in the problems cited by a much larger number, namely the difficulty in achieving the stockholders' desire that they develop a stronger and more profitable fee-earning or investment banking activity.

This issue of structure and strategy will not be resolved easily—certainly as long as international banks continue to expand and refine their own strategies in a highly competitive market. Even the most successful Euro-bank must recognise that the structure and strategy initially established by stockholders is subject to modification as the latter's own priorities, personnel and strategy evolve; for the less successful Euro-banks, change is even more likely to occur. At the same time, a large number of consortium-owned Euro-banks have avoided major changes in ownership patterns or objectives despite the changed posture of individual stockholder institutions. When such change has not taken place, constancy can be attributed to such factors as good performance in its traditional role by the existing management team, the maintenance of strong personal relationships among stockholders and between stockholders and management, or the difficulty in obtaining agreement among a large number of stockholders on a common action programme.

One of the most significant of the unresolved issues relating to Euro-banks is that of loan quality and the Euro-banker's ability to evaluate a number of types of credit which are in many respects a product of the Euro-currency market. Subsidiary to this overall issue are the ability to establish a reasonable loan loss reserve for international credits and the desirability of specialisation in some of the more popular types of geographic and sectoral loans. While other international banks confront the same issue in their sovereign risk and project lending, the relatively small size and lack of substantial retained earnings of Euro-banks coupled with their concentration on these credits makes the issue a particularly acute one for Euro-banks. Sovereign defaults are very much on the minds of Euro-bankers; six of the forty senior executives interviewed in 1979 considered this the principal issue facing them over the next few years.

The difficulty of evaluating country risk and of dealing with sovereign governments has been well described in publications by such prominent bankers as Alexander Wolfe Jr[1] and Richard Cummings.[2] In brief, Euro-banks are lending in unprecedented amounts, for unprecedented maturities, to a wide variety of countries which carry a significant economic and/or political risk. The precedents from the nineteenth and early twentieth centuries cited in Chapter 1, when private investors' funds rather than bank deposits were at risk, are not particularly encouraging. Violent price fluctuations in a few key commodities, war and civil strife and a change in form of government lead the banking historian to conclude that some country defaults are inevitable over the period of time today's 'medium-term' loans to sovereign borrowers tend to be outstanding.

Even if one's ability to evaluate sovereign risk credits were better than the current state of the art, the length of today's maturities substantially limits the flexibility which banks like Barings had in the nineteenth century when short-term facilities could be run down when trouble appeared on the horizon. Confronted with a sovereign borrower unwilling or unable to meet its obligations, the banker's best course of action is likely to be to negotiate for the best work-out possible. While most if not all of these borrowers value highly their credit rating and will make every effort to avoid a default situation, history has shown how vulnerable these intentions can be in a time of economic or political difficulty.

The second half of the 1970s has indeed borne out both the historians' prediction of future sovereign defaults as well as the relative lack of influence of the private banking community when confronted with either a defaulting government which, logically or illogically, refuses or is unable to take appropriate steps to justify a restructuring of its foreign debt or, worse, a total lack of governmental authority with which to deal. The recent experience of Turkey, Zaire, Peru and Iran demonstrates the vulnerability of bank lenders to a host of political and economic considerations which may oblige a foreign banker at a minimum to wait an extended period until a default can be corrected.

In 1975 private bankers argued that their claims would be the last to suffer in a rescheduling exercise in view of the value attached to credibility in the international private financial markets; even such a rescheduling would be preferable to the prospect of partial or total loss or principal lent to a failed private corporation or project which is not associated with the sovereign state's presumed ability and motivation to resume its role in the Euro-currency market. By 1979, however, the issue was whether reserves should be established for loans to defaulting sovereign borrowers who were either unable to negotiate a mutually agreeable debt rescheduling or incapable of servicing the newly-rescheduled debt.

The violent shifts or discontinuities in market psychology—some would say herd instinct—do not exactly instill confidence in bankers' ability to evaluate country risk. Perhaps the classic case of a borrower becoming unacceptable almost overnight in the Euro-markets was that of Italy, which moved suddenly in mid-1974 from the status of a borrower enjoying the very finest terms to one where, for various reasons, the entire market seemed to be 'full up' on Italy, with the result that official bilateral assistance became necessary. In mid-1978, Iran too was regarded as a prime borrower until suddenly the international banking community withdrew its vote of confidence.

By mid-1979, therefore, Euro-bankers had become more conscious of the vulnerability of even the more highly regarded but heavily indebted borrowers to unpredictable economic or political events which, when coupled with abrupt changes in market psychology, could freeze or immobilise a small but significant portion of a Euro-bank's sovereign loan portfolio.

Risk evaluation in private sector credits is equally if not more difficult. Although many bankers express a preference for corporate or project credits which can be better evaluated in terms of their professional training than a sovereign risk, the uncertainties for the former type of financing resulting from inflation, the size and complexity of many modern projects and changes in technology have been well described by Professor Charles Williams and others.[3] Such imponderables as the supply and demand for large oil tankers and semi-submersible oil rigs, the technological uncertainties of nuclear power and liquid natural gas systems, and the evaluation of oil under the North Sea represent levels of uncertainty reminiscent of the railway financing boom of the mid-nineteenth century which produced its share of massive cost overruns, over supply of facilities and proliferation of uneconomic projects.

Even in more traditional sectors such as real estate lending, Euro-banks have undertaken risks of which in many cases they were unaware. As mentioned earlier, significant losses have been suffered in the United Kingdom property market by Euro-banks who were aware that property values could fall as well as rise but who never foresaw the virtual disappearance for a protracted period of time in 1974–5 of the institutional market for real estate upon which so many deficit cash flow property companies relied to meet their obligations. Euro-banks have also been significant lenders to the much criticised US Real Estate Investment Trusts. While in retrospect much of this lending is subject to criticism, the number of bankers who corrected foresaw in 1972–3 the virtually complete collapse of this widely heralded new sector in 1974–5 were thin on the ground at the time. In oil tanker finance, which has also attracted Euro-bank interest, critics of the enthusiasm of bankers for a glamorous new industry which was over-expanding to meet a generally agreed level of demand should also bear in mind the almost totally unexpected impact on this demand of the October War in 1973 with its fivefold increase in oil prices.

For the majority of Euro-banks, the good old days when international lending involved self-liquidating trade finance or loans to the overseas subsidiaries of well-established multinational companies are well and truly gone. Building and maintaining a Euro-loan portfolio in large part from market sources therefore involves some exposure to a combination of sovereign and corporate/project risk which has few historical precedents.

One hesitates to draw any historical parallels with earlier periods of international banking expansion in view of the obvious differences in environment, but there are some definite parallels in sovereign risk and project lending. The Medici with Yorkist English monarchs and the Duke of Burgundy, the Fugger *vis-à-vis* the Habsburgs, and nineteenth century French and English merchant banks with various sovereigns in Egypt, Turkey, Southern Europe and Latin America all at one time or another came up against a sovereign authority who could not or would not meet its obligations. While investors rather than bankers usually suffered the loss in the nineteenth century, the number of new international banks who disappeared within a few years of their opening for business is, unfortunately, rather high.

From this issue stems the problem of establishing an adequate loan loss reserve. For the reasons given above, individual or industry-wide data provide little useful guidance. With very few exceptions, the forty Euro-banks analysed in Chapter 6 give no indication of total loan loss experience. Bankers' natural reluctance to talk about their less success-ful loans plus the paucity of reporting requirements for Euro-banks reduces one to analysing the occasional publicly available statistics which provide outstandings to a given troubled country borrower or the aggregate amount of a certain sector's borrowing in the London market.

While only a handful of Euro-banks publish complete data on loss experience and the level of loan loss reserves, a glimpse of the extent of Euro-bank loss exposure is given by the reported losses suffered by several banks in Hong Kong, Singapore and London. Of the four London banks reporting net losses in 1974 due to loan write-offs, in one case the reserve established approximated the bank's capital, while in two instances the bank's auditors felt unable to comment on the adequacy of the reserve constituted. The actual impact of losses was shifted in several other instances to parent institutions by the transfer of the assets involved. Given the relative youth of many Euro-banks and the impact even a single loss can have on a bank which has not established substantial disclosed or hidden reserves, one can understand the wide range of size of loss reserve which is cited as desirable by Euro-bank executives.

For an outsider to evaluate the loss potential of a given Euro-bank portfolio is virtually impossible. The broad industry or geographic breakdowns published by some institutions are almost meaningless from this standpoint, as only a detailed appraisal of each loan would provide a useful guide to loss exposure. What one can say, however, is that most Euro-banks have on their books loans to real estate companies, sovereign borrowers, shipowners or other private sector entities which are not accruing interest and could well represent a possible loss. This loss experience is obviously difficult to quantify given the paucity of reported data, but one possible standard of measurement is the reported international loss experience of the major US banks which in recent years has been running at ·30–·40 per cent of the international loan portfolio per annum.[4]

Another sub-issue which arises from the general problem of risk evaluation is the dilemma of diversification of risk as opposed to specialisation. The interviews reported in Chapter 3 bring out the importance most Euro-banks place on diversification. Asset controls based on country exposure, percentage of capital funds lent to a single borrower and ceilings on industry exposure play a key role in the asset management policy of most Euro-banks. In many cases, Euro-bank management seeks to involve stockholders in asset diversification decisions. Euro-bankers are well aware that a great majority of the recent international bank failures and substantial loan losses have occurred as a result of overconcentration on specific sectors such as real estate.

A contrary view, however, holds that a reasonable degree of asset specialisation is vital to the success of a Euro-bank. The natural proponents of this view are the Euro-banks whose sponsorship involves an inevitable degree of geographic or functional asset concentration. While offering their sponsors and the market the traditional advantages of specialist expertise, these banks generally regard themselves as extensions of their much larger parents and therefore able to minimise the disadvantages of overconcentration by support from financially powerful stockholders. On a more general plane, it is agreed by many Euro-bank executives that their banks can succeed in the long run only by establishing an identity distinct from their parents and other banks, and that developing specialist skills in financing growing and credit-worthy market sectors is one of the few means of achieving this identity. In many cases, such skills are a natural concomitant of the Euro-bank's management team or its stockholder connections and resources. Rather than allocate their loan portfolio to dozens of different countries whose creditworthiness they feel they can never properly evaluate or to lend to industries with which they have no real familiarity, some Euro-banks prefer to focus on sectors which may carry a high perceived level of risk or complexity but one which the banker not only feels capable of evaluating and limiting but also receives more than adequate compensation in terms of fees, deposits, loan spreads and possibly equity kickers. Unfortunately, many of the sectors in the early 1970s which attracted this strategic thinking – shipping, natural resources, real estate, and energy – suffered in 1974–5 from overcapacity, economic problems and various uncertainties, so that many Euro-banks found themselves in 1975 dismantling newly established specialist lending units.

Another major unresolved issue for Euro-banks today is the adequacy of funding sources. The theoretical problem of converting short-term deposits into financial commitments of several years or more became a very real one in the second half of 1974. The fact that Euro-banks met their obligations under extremely difficult conditions is a tribute to intelligent central bank leadership, the willingness of parent banks to provide support in a variety of forms, and persistent efforts by bankers on a personal level to modify and rationalise some of the more drastic measures taken initially by the senior management of lending banks concerned about their interbank exposure.

Success in surmounting the 1974 crisis of confidence, however, provides no assurance that a similar or more serious one in the future, perhaps accompanied more by serious loan losses rather than the spate of rumours which was often the case in 1974, will not recur. For example, five of the forty bankers interviewed in 1979 expressed the view that the greatest threat to their long term viability was a recurrence of the 1974 liquidity crisis. Channels of assistance from parent institutions have been established if not actually utilised, serious attempts are being made by many Euro-banks to diversify their sources of funds, and personal contacts and structures have been established by individual managements and dealers which should prove useful in a future funding crisis. On the other hand, the ability of a separately capitalised bank to consistently attract interbank deposits to fund long-term commitments has been called into question. Rightly or wrongly, sponsorship or ownership in 1974 and 1975 played a key role in a Euro-bank's ability to attract funds. More recently, a crisis in a country such as Iran which is the focus of a given Euro-bank's activity can be transmitted, rightly or wrongly, to that particular institution and impact its ability to attract deposits.

Perhaps the most persuasive and fundamental issue, however, is the Euro-bank's ability in the highly competitive markets of the late 1970s to earn a rate of return considered satisfactory by management and stockholders after deducting a reasonable loan loss allocation and assuming a generally acceptable level of gearing. Understandably enough, this issue of risk and reward in their bread-and-butter activity of Euro-currency lending was most often mentioned by Euro-bankers in mid-1979 as the major problem preoccupying them; a total of fourteen of the forty interviewed thus gave it top priority.

In 1975, the statistical performance of Euro-banks posed this issue in terms of whether Euro-banks could earn returns competitive with those of their stockholders. At the time, for example, the 1974 London sample's pre-tax return of fourteen per cent on net worth did not compare particularly favourably with those of the US and other banks which held their stock. In the event, however, Euro-bank performance—at least in London—improved while the record of many stockholder institutions since then has been relatively lack-lustre.

By 1979, however, the profitability issue was posed less in terms of comparability with parent institutions than whether a pure international bank given the current risk/reward relationships stemming from a borrower's market could earn an adequate return on invested funds. The relative profitability of a national bank's international function is difficult to calculate and can always be fudged by reference to services provided to domestic customers, but the Euro-bank's performance is highly visible and quantifiable.

The great majority of Euro-bankers have recognised that participation in interest-differential Euro-currency lending and, in most cases, the mainstream Euro-bond markets is unlikely to show a satisfactory return on funds invested should the market conditions prevalent in mid-1979 continue. While they do not benefit from the relatively cheap deposits associated with domestic customers and may be obliged to increase allocations to loan loss reserves, these Euro-banks do not suffer from the infrastructural costs of many domestic banks. Looking to the future, the Eurobanks which will earn relatively high returns on assets and stockholder funds will be those who are capable of originating fee-earning transactions, developing new products and moving against the tide into sectors which are neglected but offer above-average remuneration. It goes without saying that they thus have a major challenge before them in achieving a level of profitability comparable with that prevalent in major national banking markets.

Another unresolved issue is whether Euro-banks are capable of generating the investment banking or fee-based income which many bankers feel is necessary to provide an attractive rate of return, establish a distinctive identity for themselves as an international merchant bank, or achieve other agreed objectives. Ten of the forty Euro-bankers interviewed in mid-1979 regarded this as their most critical problem in the years to come. The great majority of Euro-banks are owned by commercial banks, and with few exceptions top management has a commercial banking background which is not necessarily the best training for the capital market and corporate finance activities which generate a significant amount of fee income. As discussed in Chapter 5, some of the most profitable aspects of investment banking – origination and corporate financial services – are dominated by a limited number of well-established national merchant or investment banks, and relatively few Euro-banks are likely to displace these traditional relationships.

To date, the banks which have been particularly successful in generating fee income either benefit from business obtained with the assistance of stockholders who carry on an active investment banking business or, in a limited number of instances, have engaged a highly experienced team of investment bankers at some cost to break into this type of business. In most instances, however, one has the impression that relatively few Euro-banks will derive significant profits from corporate financial services and capital market operations. For many of the remainder, the management and co-management of syndicated Euro-currency loans will provide the bulk of their fee income.

It should be recognised, however, that in the last half of the 1970s a number of Euro-banks which do not benefit from parent-generated investment banking income have succeeded in profitably penetrating certain sectors where they can compete with the established universal and investment banks. Such penetration has usually taken place in the relatively new and rapidly evolving markets such as floating rate notes and certificates of deposit, currency swaps and back-to-back loans, and Euro-bonds or private placements issued in the non-traditional currencies. Finally, it must also be borne in mind that entry into corporate finance or investment banking activities is barred to many Euro-banks whose stockholders are already active in them and have no appetite for further competition.

At the risk of repeating the obvious, one must raise one final issue for Euro-banks—that of their ability to attract and retain the key individuals who are essential to success whether the focus is on commercial or investment banking. Five of the forty bankers interviewed, for example, considered the 'people' issue as their primary concern for the future. In their minds the issues of current profitability, possible loan losses or penetration of the investment banking market were all secondary to that of having the people whose capabilities would resolve these issues.

The typical Euro-bank has a relatively small team of key management personnel and often relies on its flexibility and innovative response to succeed in competition with better known, more highly structured banks offering more services and greater financial resources. Without a handful of key people who can mobilise this more entrepreneurial framework, many Euro-banks would find it impossible to compete with the large national banks. Should the attractions of alternative careers— the security and continuity of a national bank or the attractive compensation and reputation of an established merchant or investment bank—drain talent from the Euro-banks, they will lose most of their raison d'etre.

Before concluding this chapter, it might be useful to mention a few issues which appear to have been successfully resolved by Euro-banks in recent years.

Perhaps most importantly, Euro-banks seem to have successfully managed their deposit mismatch and foreign exchange positions during extraordinarily difficult periods of sharply fluctuating interest rates and exchange parities. The concern has often been expressed that bankers, particularly the newer breed of Euro–bankers, were vulnerable to serious miscalculation in forecasting interest and exchange rates which larger and more experienced banks often got wrong. In the event, it has been the bigger national banks who have announced massive exchange losses either through unauthorised dealing or a major position turning sour. Table S, taken from the *Banker* magazine, lists some of these and other publicised banking losses during 1974; in only one of these situations was a Euro-bank directly involved.

This relatively good performance would appear to stem from a combination of relatively small size, simplicity of operation and the awareness by management that a major mismatch or exchange loss could not be tolerated given the small size of their earnings base. With few exceptions, the chief executives interviewed regard the taking of significant deposit, mismatch and exchange positions as having a low priority compared to loan income and fees earned. This does not imply, of course, that Euro-bankers have outperformed their more established competitors in money dealing operations, but rather that they are generally not prepared to take significant dealing risks and that control of a dealing room is simpler in a smaller organisation.

TABLE S   Banking Losses ($m., financial year 1974)

Name of bank	Assets less Contra Accounts	Losses	Cause
Chase Manhattan	41,143	29	Overvaluation of bond trading portfolio
Crédit Lyonnais	32,723	38	Operating loss (after tax)
Manufacturers Hanover	25,754	30(P)	Charge-off of loan to Franklin National Bank
Westdeutsche Landesbank Girozentrale	23,649	114	Foreign exchange dealings
Lloyds Bank	21,021	77	Foreign exchange losses at Lloyds Bank International's Lugano branch
Continental Illinois	19,526	12(P)	Provision against losses at London merchant banking subsidiary, Continental Illinois Limited
Swiss Bank Corporation	16,401	NA	Dealings with Sindona group of companies
Union Bank of Switzerland	12,281	56	Foreign exchange dealings
Hessische Landesbank Girozentrale	13,323	717(E)	Investment losses, including large losses incurred through subsidiary company Investitions und Handelsbank
Norddeutsche Landesbank Girozentrale	11,336	E127(E)	Investment losses, including those on loans to Rollei company
First National Bank of Boston	8,536	9	Cost of closing uncompleted foreign exchange deals arising from closure of Banque de Financement
Banque de Bruxelles	7,496	100	Foreign exchange dealings
Franklin National Bank	4,928*	E370(E)	Foreign exchange and loan losses
Grindlays	3,732	21(P)	Provision against investment losses, including $33 m. provision at merchant banking subsidiary, Brandts ($16 m. of the Brandts' provision is for

TABLE S   *(continued)*

Name of bank	Assets less Contra Accounts	Losses	Cause
			possible losses on property loans). (The Grindlays' figure includes a $5 m. tax charge on operating profits)
United Dominions Trust	3,322	61(P)	Provision against property loans
		22	Operating loss (including $3 m. tax charge)
Hill Samuel	2,729	10	Write-off of 50 % of uncompleted foreign exchange deals left after closure of Bankhaus I. D. Herstatt
Security National Bank	1,803*	E140(E)	Investment losses

Notes: Figures in local currency converted at exchange rates prevailing early May.
Loss figures are given before tax unless otherwise stated.
*These banks have now been taken over by other banks and so do not appear in this year's ranking.
(P) denotes a provision against possible losses.
(E) denotes an estimate of possible losses.
Source: *Banker* (June 1975).

Another problem with which most Euro-banks seem to have successfully dealt is the tiering, or splitting of LIBOR paid by various banks on the basis of presumed credit standing. In the context of 1974 of emphasis on credit quality, various levels of premia over LIBOR were paid by a number of Euro-banks, and the concern was expressed that this would become a permanent pricing mechanism which would substantially reduce Euro-banks' gross lending spreads. Although such premia continue to be charged to individual banks, Euro-banks as a whole have resisted paying significantly over the offered rate for funds. In addition, pricing flexibility to preserve gross margins has been created either by a Euro-bank insisting on using its own LIBOR when it lends directly to a customer or by using a blend of individual LIBOR rates, including those of smaller institutions, to price larger syndicated credits. A related issue with which the Euro-banks have successfully dealt is that of the recycling of OPEC money in 1974–5. While only a limited amount of OPEC funds has flowed directly to Euro-banks, the large US and European institutions which are the principal direct recipients of such funds have in turn recycled these funds – after taking the appropriate turn – to Euro-banks and other institutions.

8 The Outlook for Euro-Banks

An assessment of the future development for Euro-banks must take into consideration both the variables which are largely beyond the control of the bank's management and those factors which lie within their power to influence. The exogenous variables which will play a significant role in the Euro-bank's future are the state of the Euro-markets themselves and the attitudes of Euro-bank stockholders.

As by-products of the development of the Euro-markets, Euro-banks are dependent in large part on the market's size, rate of growth or decline, structure and current psychological state. Prognostications on the future of the international financial markets centred in London abound, and often, depending on the current state of sentiment, observers swing from a positive view of the Euro-market based on its growth, potential economic contribution, and institutional necessity to a negative one characterised by physical decline, transmission of inflation and other unpleasant national economic phenomena, and propagation of unsound credit practices. Over their relatively short period of existence, the Euro-markets have continued to produce great adaptability to changing circumstances, new lending techniques and practices, and an almost unchecked record of rapid growth – all of which seems to indicate that they have become a useful institution in a highly internationalised world economy. The events of the 1970s, in particular the successful recycling of OPEC surpluses, have shown how unlikely is a 'drying up' or reflow of funds to national markets. It would appear that the market actually thrives on presumably adverse developments, and dire predictions as to the future of the market are continually proven wrong.

The Euro-market's success is a function of the strength and sophistication of the money market mechanism in London and elsewhere, the ability to offer highly competitive interest rates and lending margins in a variety of currencies, geographic spread with sub-markets throughout the world, the willingness to undertake new risks and establish new credit mechanisms, and a physical capacity which rivals that of most domestic financial markets. Its vulnerability lies in its dependence on heavy borrowings from developing countries, on the existence of a certain level of confidence and, to a lesser extent, the ability of national markets to offer a competitive service to borrowers. While individual sovereign defaults will continue to occur, actual loss experience over time should not exceed the norm for most domestic economies. The almost inevitable presence of institutional and administrative barriers to the free flow of funds among national markets should ensure that the Euro-markets retain their distinctive attractions of size, sophistication, responsiveness, relative cheapness and risk preference. One cannot exclude the possibility of a 1930s-type depression and collapse of the international financial system, although the Euro-market's survival in 1974 would appear to confirm their ability to withstand stresses approaching the 1930s collapse in intensity.

The greatest threat to the market in practice has been the crisis of confidence of 1974 which resulted in a temporary significant shrinking of the interbank segment and a sharply modified risk/reward preference in the direct lending portion of the market. A similar or perhaps more serious blow to confidence in the future cannot be excluded, particularly if loss experience in the types of credits which have been popular in the Euromarket is regarded as unacceptably high. The Euro-banks would naturally be among the first to suffer from the resulting likely retrenchment of the interbank market as well as the possible direct loan losses which precipitated the decline in confidence. Given the likely support in various forms of parent banks and central banking authorities, however, the impact of such a retrenchment would probably take the form of shrunken balance sheet footings and profits and consolidation within the structure of parent banks rather than actual failures.

Inevitably the growth of the Euro-currency market will lead, even in the absence of such a crisis, to increased supervision and regulation on the part of central banking and governmental authorities. Given the difficulty of imposing rigid direct controls on such an enormous and widespread market, however, regulation is likely to take the form of indirect controls on international activities of national banks applied by the latter's central banks; such controls on international activities could include gearing limitations, 'administrative guidance' or 'jawboning' with regard to the size, profitability and composition of international loan portfolios, and ceilings placed on loans to certain types of borrowers.

Within this framework of continued development punctuated by possible declines stemming from a blow to confidence, the risk/reward ratio on Euro-currency loans, which are the backbone of most Euro-banks' business, should reflect continued overcapacity in international banking and a long term tendency towards a borrowers' market. The experience of the 1970s following sharp declines in confidence and interest in new business in mid-1970 (Penn Central) and mid-1974 (Franklin and Herstatt) seem to confirm this trend. The principal difference between the borrowers' market of 1973/74 and 1978/79 is the far greater capacity in the latter period stemming from the massive entry of newcomers into the market and new implantations of established banks. While the risk/reward ratio in international lending may alter in the banks' favour, it is quite difficult to see it returning to the post-Herstatt 1975 level for more than a limited period of time because of the commitment of so many banks to complete and put to use the international infrastructure they have established. The return to spreads and maturities in 1979 which bankers universally disavowed in 1975 is witness to the primary role played by competition and capacity rather than perceptions of credit quality and profitability in establishing risk/reward ratios.

This likely continuation of a borrowers' market will have a particularly negative impact on Euro-banks as opposed to national banks with international operations. Not only do the former suffer as pure international banks this competition over the full spectrum of their activities, but also they do not benefit from the relatively cheap deposits and profitable, long-standing customer relationships associated with domestic banking in the national markets. As relatively small banks and with capital constraints imposed by local regulatory authorities such as the Monetary Authority of Singapore and the Bank of England, Euro-banks are often at a pricing disadvantage when competing with large national banks without gearing or profitability constraints.

The second major outside variable affecting the outlook for individual Euro-banks is the strategic priorities of stockholder institutions. The rapid development of the Euro-markets has been accompanied by a significant evolution of individual parent banks' strategic priorities and objectives. Confronted with an intensification of competition and the resulting need to better define its personality and strategy, the parent of a Euro-bank inevitably re-examines the role played by its affiliates in its global strategy. Such a rationalisation quite often leads to a greater regional or functional specialisation for the

Euro-bank affiliate as the parent attempts to reduce overlap and duplication as well as establish a group identity. One of the results is the buy-out of partners in a consortium bank or the significant restructuring of a wholly-owned subsidiary so as to increase the affiliate's responsiveness to the parent's needs.

Quite apart from this trend towards greater integration in a competitive market is a change in parent priorities relating purely to its domestic environment, such as a merger, substantial domestic loan losses, capital adequacy problems or a changed perception of the priority of international vis-a-vis domestic banking. Also, a parent's international priorities may have changed over time. A European bank which took a 10 per cent share in a consortium in 1970 as its first overseas banking venture may well in 1979 have an international loan portfolio and level of banking skills which exceed those of its affiliate. A large US money centre bank which set up a wholly-owned merchant bank in 1972–3 to develop an asset mix of a non-commercial banking character in the context of rising stock market and real estate values might understandably feel in 1979 that a far greater priority is to offer a range of investment banking services to augment the return on a limited asset base.

International relationships also evolve; a stockholder grouping which made sense in the conditions of the mid-1960s could a decade later have become subordinate to, or actually conflict with, a more recent association or the parent bank's desire to establish its own identity. Finally, the actual results achieved by the Euro-bank inevitably colour the parent's attitudes. It would appear that return on invested funds, market reputation, and contribution to a programme of diversification or customer service are among the principal criteria used by parent institutions to evaluate their Euro-bank affiliates. A consistently below-target return on equity or the inability to offer successfully the desired services would thus naturally raise some questions in the parent's thinking about continued support.

Stockholder attitudes have been particularly sensitised in some cases by the gradual presumption in recent years of total balance sheet support by the market and regulatory authorities such as the Bank of England. While most stockholders of wholly-owned subsidiaries and consortium banks assumed from the outset that their reputation as responsible financial institutions required a level of support of their affiliates which went beyond that normally associated with a limited liability company, the 1974 confidence crisis and subsequent requirement by the Bank of England for letters of support rendered this assumption quite explicit for all Euro-banks operating in the London market.

For a relatively small stockholder with its own domestic problems, this clarification in some cases may well have substantially modified the stockholder's attitude to the amount and type of business being carried on by the Euro-bank affiliate.

The importance of stockholder support was brought out by the interviews analysed earlier in this book. The most immediate source of support, of course, is funding assistance. With adequate back-up facilities in the form of direct funding or the ability to sell loans to parent banks, management can not only sleep better at night but also run its dealing position more profitably in view of the lessened need to provide a full liquidity backstop. Secondly, the difficulty any new bank has in attracting deposits and quality loan business places a premium on relationships which can be provided directly or indirectly by parent institutions. Finally, in the highly competitive investment banking business, the origination and placing capability of a parent institution willing and able to pass this business and resources on to its Euro-bank affiliate can mean the difference between a successful or loss-making investment banking activity.

The trend towards greater integration of Euro-banks with parent institutions reflected in the number of buy-outs and restructurings of the 1975–9 period should continue. Of the forty banks in the London sample, there were ten instances during this time of stockholder rearrangements which resulted in the buy-out of minority interests by a majority holder or the reconstruction of equity holdings around one or two major stockholders. New Euro-banks will continue to be established in London and elsewhere, but the relatively few new institutions will have a more narrowly defined role than was the case in the 1960s and early 1970s.

Changes in stockholder objectives and priorities have often proven difficult, however, to translate into major modifications of Euro-bank ownership, structure, capital size and type of business if more than one stockholder is involved. Each stockholder invariably has its own views on the importance of profitability, the quality of management, business strategy and priorities, with the result that decisions involving the buy-out of other stockholders, changes in management, increases in capital or significant changes in business strategy have often been deferred indefinitely due to the inability to reach unanimous agreement. Subjective views of a parent bank's image and prestige have forestalled decisions to close down or substantially reduce the activities of some consortium banks, and one has the impression that a consortium bank may only be closed down in the event of such a major mishap as the incurring of losses exceeding the capital base or failure or disappearance of the parent banks.

As mentioned earlier, business contributions in the form of introductions to corporate lending and deposit customers as well as placing power for affiliates engaged in the Euro-bond business have enabled several Euro-bank subsidiaries and affiliates of US and Continental European banks to show returns on assets and capital funds well in excess of the Euro-bank average. Looking to the future, therefore, Euro-banks with parents willing and able to provide substantial funding, new business, deposit clientele and placing power are extremely well placed to succeed in the highly competitive Euro-markets.

In addition to these exogenous variables which help determine the outlook of the Euro-bank, there are those factors which can be influenced to a greater or lesser extent by management itself.

It is, of course, stating the obvious to point out that quality of management is a vital factor in the success of a bank. Management quality is particularly relevant, however, in a highly competitive market with hundreds of banks seeking the same qualified personnel, cheap and reliable deposit base, low risk—high quality loans and loyal placing power.

As in most financial institutions, a variety of general management qualities are important to a Euro-bank's success: ability to recruit, organise and motivate staff, develop good accounting and management information systems, control expenses, establish and implement a strategic plan, maintain good relationships with other banks and so forth. But there would seem in today's Euro-markets to be five critical variables within management's control which will have a major bearing on a Euro-bank's likely performance. On this performance will turn such vital questions as a Euro-bank's reputation in the market, with its resulting impact on factors such as the ability to attract interbank deposits and to syndicate loans, the view of regulatory authorities, and its acceptance and support by stockholders, who are vitally concerned with such questions as market image, profitability and ability to provide specialist services.

The first of these variables is the ability to generate quality business for the Euro-bank's own loan portfolio and for syndication to others. While acceptable risks and adequate returns can be achieved by a passive policy of only taking loan participations from other banks, over an extended period of time the incremental return from front end origination fees coupled with the enhanced market reputation associated with a bank known for originating and managing quality business may well mean the difference between a successful and an average Euro-bank. Total or primary reliance on loans syndicated by other banks often implies a less intimate knowledge of the customer, lack of access to the most attractive business which is likely to be retained by the originating bank, and often a lower return on loan exposure. A useful deposit relationship also often accompanies own-originated business.

In the extremely competitive Euro-markets, the more highly regarded public and private borrowers are heavily solicited by literally hundreds of international banks, many of which offer services and capabilities beyond the reach of Euro-banks. Long standing personal and corporate relationships in this context play a key role, and the more successful Euro-banks are either able to benefit from a long standing relationship between a customer and a stockholder bank or from a personal connection between one of its own management personnel and the client.

A second variable is management's ability to evaluate credits and minimise loan losses. While a truism for banks in general, it is particularly vital for Euro-banks which do not have the benefit of a cushion of many years of retained earnings, operate on relatively thin gross interest margins, and depend to such an extent on the goodwill of other banks for deposits at a market cost. Not only can a single loan loss wipe out one or more years of a Euro-bank's earnings, but the psychological impact of such a loss, particularly during a period of market nervousness, may well seriously impair the bank's ability to obtain interbank funds. Loan losses experienced in 1974 by several wholly-owned London subsidiaries of American banks resulted in the change of senior management and complete restructuring of the bank's mission, usually away from a major direct lending role towards an investment banking concept. In this vital function of credit evaluation, the Euro-bank executive is confronted more than most bankers by the classic conflict of credit judgement and the need to generate new business.

The ability to earn significant fee and other non-interest related income is another variable which, as in the case of new business generation in the lending sector, will in many cases make the difference between an acceptable and an outstanding Euro-bank performance. While many Euro-banks have only recently begun to emphasise this type of income, the relative difficulty of attracting investment banking clients and the unique skills often required in successfully offering corporate financial and other fee-earning services would seem to indicate that only a fairly limited number of Euro-banks will be more than moderately successful in this business. The successful ones are likely to be those who will either inherit business and perhaps human skills from parent institutions or hire the limited number of qualified investment bankers prepared to leave a prestigious domestic investment bank in favour of a Euro-bank.

A fourth variable is the ability in a highly competitive market to maximise the revenue/operating cost ratio. With gross margins in so many cases limited by competition on new business and prepayments of older loans, controlling operating expenses assumes an importance it did not have earlier when the Euro-bank was growing rapidly and the focus was on building revenues. With personnel and premises in large part relatively fixed, the focus will be on evaluating the profitability of individual departments and customer relationships.

The final variable is management ability to establish a corporate personality and develop a market niche through the exploitation of specialist expertise in one or more chosen sectors of interest. Competing with the national banks which are invariably larger, offer a broader range of services and have long established customer ties, the typical Euro-bank must specialise to survive unless it functions solely as an adjunct to the parent organisation. Such specialisation may be regional or functional, but it must result in market recognition of a highly competitive level of expertise and track record in the chosen sectors.

An analysis of these variables in the light of experience to date and interviews with chief executives point to a number of likely general trends for Euro-banks over the next few years. First, the Euro-currency market itself, as a highly efficient alternative to national markets, should continue to expand albeit at a slower percentage rate than in its salad days of the late 1960s and early 1970s. It will, however, be subject to periodic lapses of confidence stemming from anticipated or actual problems such as dealing losses or sovereign risk defaults. Within this growing market, Euro-banks will continue to expand but may well lose market share in favour of the large national banks which dominate the sector. During periods of crisis, Euro-banks will suffer particularly in view of their relatively small size and uncertainty in some cases of source of support. Individual Euro-banks will be set up *de novo*, restructured and absorbed by parents as they have in the past, but the emphasis in most cases will be on greater specialisation and integration with parent institutions. In an increasing number of cases, the Euro-bank as an operating entity will become undistinguishable from the parent institution even though it has a separate capital, Board of Directors and dealing capability. Such proxies or substitutes for branches will reflect not only the need in given markets for regulatory or other reasons to operate through a subsidiary as opposed to a branch but also the increasing functional specialisation of the Euro-bank.

Secondly, within this overall context, several trends in profitability will become evident. As a general proposition, the average return on Euro-bank assets will reflect the intense competition and deteriorating risk/reward ratio prevalent in international banking and may well decline below the domestic profitability of their parent national banks. While a recovery in the risk/reward ratio may well occur as it did in 1970 and 1974 following a general reassessment of international lending risk, it is difficult to forecast a return to the levels of 1975–6 in view of the increased structural capacity in the sector.

As in the past, the profitability of individual banks will largely be a function of the level of loan losses and non-performing loans as well as their relative ability to generate significant fee or investment banking income either from lending or corporate finance activities. Those performing below the mean are, therefore, likely to be victims of loan losses which will have a particularly strong impact on those Euro-banks which have not built up internal reserves sufficient to cushion the shock of a bad loan. Whereas the damage done to Euro-banks in the mid-1970s was attributable largely to sour real estate and shipping loans, in the years to come loss exposure may also stem from the possibility of loss on a sovereign or quasi-sovereign risk exposure.

On the other hand, the outstanding performers in the future are likely to be the relatively small handful of banks in a position to earn significant non-interest income from the origination of Euro-currency loan syndications and investment banking transactions. These are likely to include the subsidiaries of large US, Scandinavian, Japanese and Continental banks which represent the loan syndication arms of their parents as well as engage in a significant amount of commercial and investment banking business directed to them by the parent. It must be borne in mind, of course, that reported earnings of several of these Euro-banks reflect not only the asset, customer, placing power and other strengths of the parent organisation, but may also be the product of arbitrary allocations of income and expense to the affiliate which in most cases is a wholly-owned subsidiary.

In addition to these 'flagship' affiliates of larger national banks, Euro-banks which specialise in generating loans from active borrowing sectors such as Latin America, Eastern Europe and the energy sector should also enjoy high returns during the period in which these sectors are particularly active.

In an effort to maximise profitability in the face of rising operating costs and declining or stable gross interest margins, Euro-bank management can be expected to take a number of internal policy measures. First, many banks will continue to reduce the portion of assets placed with other banks to increase the overall return on assets. While lip service may be paid to the desirability of operating on both sides of the market, profit pressures will oblige many banks to rely to a greater extent on parent institutions for liquidity. Secondly, attempts to cut operating costs may result in such measures as hiring freezes, efforts to reduce overhead and rental expense, and the reduction or closing of relatively unprofitable departments or offices. Finally, in an effort to raise the average yield of their loan portfolio, Euro-banks will regulate perhaps more than most national banks the addition of new business at interest spreads regarded during the borrowers' market of 1978–9 as totally inadequate to achieve an acceptable return on capital and assets. The use of increased gearing to achieve the latter objective offers relatively little scope in view of the pressures applied by regulatory authorities and stockholders in recent years.

A third trend for Euro-banks will be the rationalisation of types of activity. Until the mid-1970s, most Euro-banks opened up with the advertised intention of providing a full range of commercial and investment banking activities. The growing international operations of many parent institutions and the actual performance of their Euro-bank affiliates will lead to a narrowing of this product range in most instances. Greater concern will be focused on an individual bank's identity to differentiate it from parent and competitor institutions as well as providing a competitive business strategy. On the other hand, a number of the larger, older Euro-banks set up as medium-term lending institutions have already established their own momentum and identity in this sector and will continue to specialise in medium-term loans. Other institutions organised to channel funds to and from specific geographic or functional areas will retain this role as long as this flow of funds continues; if the need declines significantly, however, a change in strategy may be dictated. Finally, those Euro-banks established essentially as branches of full service parents to participate in a broad range of Euromarket activities will probably continue to offer a wide gamut of services.

In the case of many wholly-owned and consortium Euro-banks, however, lending activities will be regarded by parent institutions as duplicating or competing with those of the parents. In such cases, these banks will increasingly focus on fee-earning or investment/merchant banking activities which represent a useful diversification move for the stockholders. Profitability may well play a significant role in determining product line. On the one hand, management and stockholders may regard Euro-currency lending as a marginally profitable business and prefer to focus on other activities. On the other hand, the difficulties of personnel recruitment, developing placing power, and acquisition of quality corporate finance business may lead other banks to close down their Euro-bond or corporate finance departments as an economy measure to focus on banking business. Such decisions will depend on the ability of stockholders to provide assistance, the Euro-bank's track record, and management's own strengths and weaknesses.

In each of the trends can be seen the critical importance of the attitude of stockholders. In the case of consortium banks with a large number of stockholders, dissatisfaction by individual stockholders with the rate of return achieved and the services offered by the Euro-bank may not be translated into action because of the inability to reach unanimous agreement with other stockholders. On the other hand, the major ownership restructuring of a number of consortium banks in the late 1970s reflects the desire of parent banks to have a meaningful stake in an affiliate responsive to their global strategy; if such objectives cannot be achieved, they would prefer to divest themselves of their equity interest.

Even if major problems of funding or loan quality are encountered by a consortium bank, the consensus decision can be expected to be support and restructuring rather than liquidation. In one case of publicly acknowledged funding problems of a Euro-bank in 1974, that of Western American Bank, a major consortium bank, stockholders were prepared to buy a major portion of the bank's loan portfolio. In other cases, Euro-bank management by its personality and performance record may create a momentum and identity which stockholders prefer to retain as the most practicable course of action. Probably the greatest structural change, therefore, will be observed in wholly-owned subsidiaries where profit record, change in parent circumstances or objectives and relative ability to develop a useful range of services for the parent bank will largely determine whether the subsidiary Euro-bank will follow the line of development initially envisaged.

These wholly-owned subsidiaries can be restructured more easily than consortium organisations, although as in the case of the latter the parent's sensitivity to its market image may well result in the maintenance of a higher and broader level of activity than would otherwise be the case.

As indicated earlier, stockholders appear to evaluate their Euro-bank affiliates not only in terms of profitability but also in those of market reputation, the providing·of a specific range of services to supplement those of the stockholders, and an association with a desirable group of co-stockholders. Thus, an unprofitable investment banking division of a Euro-bank affiliate may well appear justified to an ownership group composed of commercial banks.

The physical location of Euro-banks has traditionally been a subject of great speculation, as potentially attractive traditional financial centres such as New York or completely new markets such as Singapore and Bahrain appear to threaten London's post-war dominance of the Euro–markets. The analysis in this volume has focused on Euro-banks active primarily in the London market because of the latter's physical and structural importance as well as the collective and individual importance of the Euro-banks based in London. Such an analysis undoubtedly does not give a full perspective on the operation of Euro-banks worldwide, although the issues described are generic ones for the sector regardless of location. While London's market share may decline further in the coming years due to the undoubted advantages of other financial centres such as market proximity, time differentials, and lower taxes or operating expenses, under present conditions a bank which wishes to participate actively in the international lending and deposit market must give London at least serious consideration before setting up a new organisation.

Individual Euro-banks may well move part or all of their corporate structure and operations from London in the future because of tax and operating cost advantages. A major shift of the Euro-markets out of London, however, would seem to require not only a significant deterioration of present operating conditions in the London market but also an attractive alternative. Should such a mass movement occur, however, one can assume that the present London market with all its advantages of communication, regulatory climate and presence of hundreds of market makers will be re-established in a single new centre rather than be scattered throughout the world.

In the meantime, regional centres such as Hong Kong and Bahrain will continue to thrive on the basis of their proximity to major regional markets, time differentials, cost advantages and other factors. Each of these markets, however, will continue to look to London for the foreseeable future as the major loan syndication centre and source of ultimate funds availability.

As a concluding note on this glimpse into the future, it is appropriate to summarise some conclusions drawn from the experience of earlier international banks and market structures going back to the Renaissance period. From an admittedly limited exploration of the published literature on early international banking, one notes a number of recurring themes which have led to the downfall of individual banks established to do international business. As so many Euro-bankers recognised during the troubles of 1974, simple survival is a precondition to achieving the lofty goals usually established for Euro-banks at their foundation, and survival for many Euro-banks was a very real issue during the events of the mid-1970s.

Looking to the future survival potential of Euro-banks on the basis of the experiences described in Chapter 1, one immediately is aware of the vital impact of political and economic events such as war and recession on the ability of international banks to survive, much less achieve stated objectives. The global recession of 1974–5 has made today's bankers more aware of their vulnerability to such events, and in the future Euro-bankers would be wise to build into their decision-making process the likelihood of at least an occasional economic or political disaster beyond their control with its consequent impact on sovereign risk, commodity, project and other loans.

Secondly, the theme of overconcentration of risk runs throughout the history of international banking disasters. Whether it be a particular sovereign risk or industrial sector, countless international banks have come unstuck because of overenthusiasm for a particular type of business. Once again, the recent problems of some of the more popular borrowing sectors in 1972–3 should bring home to international bankers in the future the possible correlation between current popularity and future oversupply and other problems. In the late 1970s, the concentration of lending to certain sovereign borrowers who 'could not afford to default' may have sown the seeds of future problems for individual banks.

A final theme relates to the quality of international bank management itself. In the past, experienced and inexperienced bankers alike were thrown into novel overseas lending situations involving less developed countries and financial structures as well as totally different types of risk and credit evaluation. Compounding these structural difficulties was the natural enthusiasm of the management of a new institution to make its own mark. Conditions in today's international markets are not significantly different, and the Euro-banker of today would do well to remind himself that he is building for the very long term and that opportunities which may appear attractive in the short term may jeopardise his survival. A subsidiary theme in the management issue is the extent and quality of guidance from home office or parent institutions. International banking history is replete with the failures of overseas subsidiaries or branches left to carry on alone without some form of surveillance from stockholders' representatives.

Notes

Introduction and Overview

1 Paul Einzig, *Roll-over Credits – The System of Adaptable Interest Rates* (London, 1973); Geoffrey Bell, *The Euro-dollar Market and the International Financial System* (London, 1973); Brian Scott Quinn, *The New Euro-markets* (London, 1975); and *Offshore Lending by US Commercial Banks*, a publication of the Robert Morris Associates and the Bankers' Association for Foreign Trade (Philadelphia, 1975).

Chapter 1

1 Richard Ehrenberg, *Capital and Finance in the Age of the Renaissance* (London, 1928) p. 103.
2 Raymond de Roover, *The Rise and Decline of the Medici Bank* (Cambridge, Mass., 1963) p. 47.
3 Ibid., p. 95.
4 Ibid., p. 121.
5 Ibid., p. 264.
6 Ibid., p. 5.
7 Ibid., p. 372.
8 Ehrenberg, pp. 268, 270, 275.
9 Ibid., p. 93.
10 Ibid., pp. 103–4.
11 Ibid., p. 131.
12 Ralph Hidy, *The House of Baring in American Trade and Finance* (Cambridge, Mass., 1949).
13 Ibid., p. 146.
14 David Joslin, *A Century of Banking in Latin America* (London, 1963).
15 J. A. Henry, *The First Hundred Years of the Standard Bank* (London, 1963).
16 E. C. Corti, *The Reign of the House of Rothschild* (New York, 1928) p. 63.
17 Ibid., pp. 110–12.
18 Ibid., p. 174.
19 Rondo Cameron, 'The Crédit Mobilier and the Economic Development of Europe', *Journal of Political Economy* (Dec. 1953).
20 Ibid., p. 470.
21 Ibid., p. 485.
22 L. H. Jenks, *Migration of British Capital to 1875* (London, 1927) p. 282.
23 Ibid., p. 49.
24 D. S. Landes, *Bankers and Pashas* (London, 1958) p. 52.

25 Victor Allen, 'The Prince of Poyais', *History Today* (Jan. 1959).
26 Jenks, pp. 256–9.
27 Ibid., p. 291–2.
28 A. J. S. Baster, *The International Banks* (London, 1935) p. 61.
29 Ibid., p. 68.
30 Ibid., p. 165.
31 Ibid., p. 48.
32 Ibid., p. 40.
33 Herbert Feis, *Europe, the World's Banker: 1870–1914* (New Haven, Conn., 1930) pp. 14, 16, 23.
34 Ibid., p. 210.
35 Clyde W. Phelps, *The Foreign Expansion of American Banks* (New York, 1927) p. 20.
36 Ibid., p. 131.
37 Ibid., p. 37; quotation from H. P. Willis, *Federal Reserve System* (New York, 1923) p. 1229.
38 Phelps, p. 164.
39 Siegfried Stern, *The United States in International Banking* (New York, 1951).
40 Ibid., p. 217.
41 Ibid., p. 224.
42 Hal B. Lary, *The United States in the World Economy*, US Department of Commerce (Washington, 1943).

Chapter 2

1 BIS, *49th Annual Report* for period ending 31 March 1979, p. 118.
2 Morgan Guaranty Trust Co., *World Financial Markets* (New York, 1979).
3 *The Economist*, 2 June 1979, p. 83.
4 'International Capital Transactions of the US' *Federal Reserve Bulletin* (June 1975) Table 19a.
5 *Banker* (Nov. 1978) p. 65.
6 Bank of England ECI (28 Nov. 1978) and *Contributions to UK Banking Statistics* (Jan. 1979)
7 *Bank of England Quarterly Bulletin*, vol. 19, no. 1, Mar. 1979
8 *Luxembourg as a Financial Centre*, published by the Commissariat au Control des Banques, 1979.
9 *The Monetary Authority of Singapore Quarterly Bulletin*, 1st Quarter 1979, vol. 7, no. 1.
10 *Who is Where in World Banking*, The Banker Research Unit 1979.
11 George Blunden, 'The Supervision of the UK Banking System', *Bank of England Quarterly Bulletin* (June 1975) p. 188.
12 'Foreign Banks in London', *Banker* (Nov. 1978).

Chapter 3

1 Steven I. Davis, *The Management Function in International Banking* (Macmillan, 1979) p. 95.

Chapter 4

1 BIS *49th Annual Report*, p. 118.
2 'The Capital and Liquidity Adequacy of Banks', *Bank of England Quarterly Bulletin* (Sep. 1975) p. 240.

Chapter 5

1 World Bank Group, *Borrowing in International Capital Markets* (Washington, 1979) EC-181/752.
2 Morgan Guaranty Trust Co., *World Financial Markets*.

Chapter 7

1 Alexander Wolfe Jr, 'Country Risk', Chapter 2 in *Offshore Lending by US Commercial Banks* (the Robert Morris Associates and the Bankers' Association for Foreign Trade (Philadelphia, 1979).
2 Richard Cummings, 'International Credits—Milestones or Millstones', *Journal of Commercial Bank Lending* (Jan. 1975).
3 Professor Charles Williams, Chapter 13 in *Offshore Lending by US Commercial Banks*, op. cit.
4 Steven I. Davis, *The Management Functions in International Banking* (Macmillan, 1979) p. 95.

Index